The 20th Century's

Most Influential

HISPANICS

Diego Rivera
Muralist

by Kevin Hillstrom

LUCENT BOOKS

A part of Gale, Cengage Learning

GALE
CENGAGE Learning™

Detroit • New York • San Francisco • New Haven, Conn • Waterville, Maine • London

LIBRARY OF CONGRESS CATALOGING-IN-PUBLICATION DATA

Hillstrom, Kevin, 1963-
  Diego Rivera : muralist / By Kevin Hillstrom.
    p. cm. -- (The twentieth century's most influential Hispanics)
  Includes bibliographical references and index.
  ISBN-13: 978-1-4205-0018-9 (hardcover)
  1. Rivera, Diego, 1886-1957--Juvenile literature. 2. Painters--Mexico--Biography-- Juvenile literature. I. Title.
  ND259.R5H55 2007
  759.972--dc22
  [B]
                                                                2007032104

Lucent Books
27500 Drake Rd
Farmington Hills MI 48331

ISBN-13: 978-1-4205-0018-9
ISBN-10: 1-4205-0018-X

Printed in the United States of America
1 2 3 4 5 6 7 12 11 10 09 08

Table of Contents

Foreword

Hispanics in America and elsewhere have shed humble beginnings to soar to impressive and previously unreachable heights. In the twenty-first century, influential Hispanic figures can be found worldwide and in all fields of endeavor including science, politics, education, the arts, sports, religion, and literature. Some accomplishments, like those of musician Carlos Santana or author Alisa Valdes-Rodriguez, have added a much-needed Hispanic voice to the artistic landscape. Others, such as revolutionary Che Guevara or labor leader Dolores Huerta, have spawned international social movements that have enriched the rights of all peoples.

But who exactly is Hispanic? When studying influential Hispanics, it is important to understand what the term actually means. Unlike strictly racial categories like "black" or "Asian," the term "Hispanic" joins a huge swath of people from different countries, religions, and races. The category was first used by the U.S. census bureau in 1980 and is used to refer to Spanish-speaking people of any race. Officially, it denotes a person whose ancestry either descends in whole or in part from the people of Spain or from the various peoples of Spanish-speaking Latin America. Often the term "Hispanic" is used synonymously with the term "Latino," but the two actually have slightly different meanings. "Latino" refers only to people from the countries of Latin America, such as Argentina, Brazil, and Venezuela, whether they speak Spanish or Portuguese. Meanwhile, Hispanic refers only to Spanish-speaking peoples but from any Spanish-speaking country, such as Spain, Puerto Rico, or Mexico.

In America, Hispanics are reaching new heights of cultural influence, buying power, and political clout. More than 35 million people identified themselves as Hispanic on the 2000 U.S. census, and there were estimated to be more than 41 million Hispanics in America as of 2006. In the twenty-first century people of Hispanic origin have officially become the nation's largest ethnic minority, outnumbering both blacks and Asians. Hispanics constitute about 13 percent of the nation's total population, and by 2050 their numbers are expected to rise to 102.6 million, at which point they would account for 24 percent of the total population. With growing numbers and expanding influence, Hispanic leaders, artists, politicians, and scientists in America and in other countries are commanding attention like never before.

These unique and fascinating stories are the subjects of *The Twentieth Century's Most Influential Hispanics* collection from Lucent Books. Each volume in the series critically examines the challenges, accomplishments, and legacy of influential Hispanic figures; many of whom, like Alberto Gonzales, sprang from modest beginnings to achieve groundbreaking goals. *The Twentieth Century's Most Influential Hispanics* offers vivid narrative, fully documented primary and secondary source quotes, a bibliography, thorough index, and mix of color and black-and-white photographs which enhance each volume and provide excellent starting points for research and discussion.

Introduction

Fascinating Person and Artist

Diego Rivera had a profound and lasting influence on art in North America. His work helped revive the tradition of mural painting, and the content of his frescoes encouraged other artists to create works with bold social and political content. Rivera's belief that art should be accessible to all members of society also influenced his peers and later generations of artists. This conviction also led him to leave his amazing collection of pre-Conquest Mexican art to the people of Mexico after his death. Today, this collection ranks as one of the most important historic art collections in all of Latin America.

A Great Artist, a Flawed Person

Throughout much of his life, Diego Rivera's artistic triumphs were overshadowed by the turmoil that surrounded his personal life. This became especially true in the decades after his death in 1957. During those years, Rivera's artistic legacy sometimes received less attention than his radical political views, his atheistic outlook, his habit of weaving lies into his personal history, and his long and sordid record of sexual activity.

Diego Rivera helped to revive the tradition of mural painting and his work had a profound influence on art across the world.

In many ways, this public fascination with Rivera's political and personal adventures was understandable. As one biographer observed, the painter's life was full of contradictions:

> Rivera was one of the great defenders of the Mexican Revolution, but he remained safely in Europe for most of the duration of that bloody upheaval (1910-1920). He became a propagandist for international Communism but painted a mural for the San Francisco Stock Exchange, another in Detroit financed by the family of Henry Ford, and a third for Rockefeller Center. He was one of the Big Three of Mexican muralism (along with David Alfaro Siqueiros and José Clemente Orozco), expressing occasionally savage visions of class and ethnic exploitation in Mexico. But he earned handsome fees for his easel paintings of society women. . . . He joined, then left, the

Communist Party and sponsored Trotsky's exile in Mexico; but in later life, he humbled himself to gain readmission to the Party at a time when everyone knew Joseph Stalin was a monster. Diego Rivera was, in short, a man of his times, with all their passions and contradictions.[1]

Rivera's exploits have been a subject of particular interest. This interest is partly due to Rivera's overweight and homely appearance, which made him an unlikely sex symbol. But fascination with this part of Rivera's life also is due to the fact that many of the glamorous women who fell under his spell expressed lifelong affection and admiration for the painter. "He was monumentally self-absorbed," observed one writer. "But women to whom he had been abusive seemed to harbor a mysterious affection for him. No doubt it partly had to do with what we see in his art, which is a humanity not readily apparent in his personal dealings. Rivera exemplifies the fact that great artists aren't necessarily (in fact, are rarely) great people."[2]

Devoted to His Art

Many of the women who became romantically involved with Rivera commented that no single woman could compete with his painting for the artist's attention. Frida Kahlo, whose life was intertwined with Rivera's for a quarter-century, often told friends and family members that the only great passion in Rivera's life was his art. Historians and biographers have offered similar assessments. "Rivera was a very serious man about only one thing in the world: his art," wrote one scholar. "Into it he poured all his mental and physical resources, from childhood on."[3]

Painting was important to Rivera because it was the most effective tool he had for communicating with the world around him. His murals, easel paintings, and sketches tell the world about the things that mattered to him, and tell the people of Mexico and other nations about his strong political, religious, and social beliefs. Rivera's art clearly shows that he was "a painter who loved his country and his people."[4] Rivera also believed that art belonged to all the people, not just the wealthy or politically powerful.

This belief led Rivera to create art that portrayed peasants, factory workers, soldiers, and other ordinary citizens as the foundations of modern society—and as people who could create a better world if they were empowered to do so. This conviction naturally led him to support communism and its vision of a society without class distinctions. Rivera's interest in creating art for the poor and working class was also instrumental in turning him toward mural making, the art form that brought him his greatest level of fame. "For him, the frescoes' size and public accessibility was the perfect canvas on which to tackle the grand themes of the history and future of humanity."[5]

The Anahuacalli Collection

Rivera's efforts as a collector of pre-Conquest art are also part of his legacy. Many of the nearly 60,000 pieces that the painter collected during the last two decades of his life would have otherwise been lost forever. Scholars say that his collection has helped them understand Mayan, Aztec, and other civilizations that existed across Central America prior to European settlement.

Some of the imagery in Rivera's paintings, which are based on his research and collection of pre-Conquest art, have even been credited with popularizing Aztec and Mayan images among the peoples of North America. As scholar Betty Ann Brown observed, "if you have seen images of the pre-Columbian world on a streetside mural in East Los Angeles, or on a restaurant menu, or on a souvenir box, odds are they were derived from the work of Diego Rivera, rather than from pre-Columbian originals."

Rivera was enormously proud of this collection, which he stored in an Aztec-styled museum known as Anahuacalli. This museum, which was completed after Rivera's death under the guidance of his daughter, Ruth, still exists today. Its collection, which includes ancient masks, sculptures, funeral urns, and other items, remains one of the most important in all of Central America.

Rivera's Murals

Most of the murals that Rivera painted in his native land showed a deep appreciation for the dignity of the Mexican people, and especially the Native Indians whose culture had been forever changed by the Spanish Conquest of the sixteenth century. But many of the frescoes he painted in Mexico also included politically charged condemnations of "abuse of power in all sectors including government, the church, and industry."[6]

The famous frescoes that Rivera painted in the United States in the early 1930s included these elements, but they also included a great deal of imagery about the modern industrial age and the impact of technology on future societies. These themes emerged as a direct result of Rivera's exposure to the skyscrapers, bridges, and other architectural marvels that he saw in America during his travels. "In all the constructions of man's past—pyramids, Roman roads and aqueducts, cathedrals and palaces—there is nothing to equal these,"[7] Rivera declared. Rivera's unique vision of American society in the industrial age was unveiled most spectacularly in *Detroit Industry*, a set of murals he completed in 1932.

Rivera's mural work also ushered in a new age of mural making, both in his native Mexico and in the United States. This mural movement also was driven by José Clemente Orozco and David Alfaro Siqueiros—the other two members of the "Big Three" brotherhood of Mexican muralists. Rivera, however, was easily the most famous of the three men during the 1930s and 1940s, and it was his work in the United States that led the federal government to fund an entire public works program devoted to creating murals.

Chapter 1

Born to Be an Artist

The enduring art that Mexican painter Diego Rivera created during his long career was deeply influenced by his childhood experiences. Diego inherited his father's commitment to helping people fight poverty and discrimination. In addition, his painting style and philosophy was shaped to a significant degree in his early years. The works that made him famous around the world reflected not only the formal instruction he received, but also the vibrant Mexican culture and landscapes through which he roamed as a youngster.

Happiness and Heartache

Diego and his twin brother José Carlos were born on December 8, 1886, into a family scarred by personal loss and political frustration. They were born in Guanajuato, an old silver mining town that was the capital of the Mexican state of the same name. His parents were Diego Rivera Sr., a school administrator and contributor to a liberal newspaper, and María del Pilar Barrientos, who was 15 years younger than her husband.

Diego later claimed that his full name at birth was Diego María de la Concepción Juan Nepomuceno Estanislao de la Rivera y Barriento Acosta y Rodríquez. Many scholars, however, believe that this fanciful name was the artist's invention. If so, it was one of many falsehoods that the artist spread about his childhood after he became famous. As one artist who knew Rivera later admitted, "he was a charming companion, a fascinating storyteller, and a compulsive liar. The full and correct details of his life may never be known, thanks to the many untruths with which he salted the record."[8]

Whatever his birth name was, both Diego and his twin brother were received into the Rivera household with great joy. Their twenty-two-year-old mother had lost three previous babies at birth, so she doted on her infant sons. Their father was delighted as well. "After each [of the family's previous children] was born dead, my father had gone out and bought my mother a doll to console her," Rivera recalled in his autobiography. "Now he did not buy a doll but cried with delight."[9]

The delivery was a grueling one for the mother, however. She lost so much blood during childbirth that she slipped into a coma and Rivera Sr. became convinced that he would have to raise his boys as a widower. María slowly recovered, though, to her husband's great relief.

The Rivera family spent the next eighteen months living peacefully in a big three-story stone house in one of Guanajuato's nicer neighborhoods. This tranquil scene was shattered by the sudden death of Diego's twin brother. The loss shook his mother's previously strong Catholic faith and pushed her to the verge of a nervous breakdown. "My mother developed a terrible neurosis, installed herself beside his tomb, and refused to leave," Diego remembered.

> My father, then a municipal councilor, was obliged to rent a room in the home of the caretaker of the cemetery in order to be with her at night. The doctor warned my father that unless my mother's mind was distracted by some kind of work, she would become a lunatic.[10]

Encouraged by her husband, María enrolled at the state's school of medicine to take courses in obstetrics, the study of pregnancy and childbirth. After earning her degree, she began working as a midwife. In 1891, she gave birth to a daughter, María del Pilar.

Life Under the Rule of Díaz

The arrival of Diego's baby sister came at a time when the economic and political fortunes of Diego Rivera Sr. were changing for the worse. Diego's father held political beliefs that were not very popular in Guanajuato. Both as a member of the town's city council and in articles he wrote for a liberal weekly paper called El Demócrata, Rivera Sr. called on the national government to provide greater economic and educational assistance to the nation's many poor people. He also believed that the

Rivera spent his childhood in Mexico when the country was ruled by Porfirio Díaz.

government needed to make democratic reforms that would give ordinary Mexicans a greater voice in shaping the nation's direction. Rivera was especially saddened at the plight of native Indians who had been pushed to the margins of Mexican society by *criollos* (Mexicans of "pure" European descent) and the growing Mexican majority of *mestizos* (Mexicans of mixed European and Indian heritage).

These beliefs put Diego's father at odds with the governing philosophy of Porfirio Díaz (1830-1915), who ruled Mexico from 1876 to 1911. They also aroused the anger and suspicion of the dictator's supporters, which included most wealthy Mexicans, the Catholic Church, and ordinary citizens who were comforted by Díaz's emphasis on law and order.

Díaz had first emerged as a national figure in the 1850s, when he and another famous figure in Mexican history, Benito Juárez (1806-1872), led a movement to topple dictator Antonio López de Santa Anna (1794-1876) from power. This liberal revolution forced Santa Anna to flee the country in 1855, and two years later the nation's new rulers adopted a new constitution. This 1857 document contained many democratic reforms, including severe restrictions on the political power of the Catholic Church and its conservative allies.

Outraged at this development, Mexican conservatives convinced France to deploy French troops to Mexico and install Archduke Maximilian (1832-1867) as emperor of the nation. The conservatives believed that if the French could seize control of the country, the Church's rightful place would be restored and the liberal threat to their wealth and lifestyle would be removed. Juárez, Díaz, and their millions of followers refused to yield, though, and in 1867, France finally withdrew after years of bloodshed. Maximilian was executed on June 19, 1867, leaving Juárez as the undisputed president of Mexico.

The Rise of Díaz

In 1871 Díaz turned against his old ally, urging his countrymen to overthrow Juárez. The following year, on July 17, Juárez died of a heart attack. Four years of political instability followed until November 21, 1876, when Díaz and his rebel army marched into Mexico City to formally claim power. This marked the beginning of the "Porfiriato"—Díaz's thirty-five-year reign over Mexico.

After seizing power, Díaz abandoned all the liberal principles for which he had fought during the previous two decades. He used threats and violence to suppress political opposition. One of the chief weapons Díaz used to frighten his countrymen into following him was the *rurales*. This police force patrolled the countryside armed with orders to stamp out any signs of rebellion from poor native Indians.

Assisted by a group of businessmen and other advisors known as *los científicos* (the scientists), Díaz also imposed a philosophy of government that emphasized large-scale foreign investment and the creation of huge wealth-generating estates called *haciendas* that were operated by political allies. The government left the poor to fend for themselves. Finally, he reached a treaty of sorts with Catholic leaders. In return for their support, he permitted the Church leadership take back some of its lost authority over Mexican society.

Curious and Creative

As a young boy, Diego was unaware of the violence, tension, and injustice that plagued his nation. Instead he spent each day in the safe and comfortable surroundings of home, where his intelligence and curiosity was nurtured. Tutored by his father, who had an extensive book collection, he learned to read at age four. He also spent hours taking toys and tools apart to see how they worked, and displayed a keen interest in trains and other large machines around the city. His fascination with machinery was so great that family members nicknamed him "the engineer."[11]

Young Diego also was, by all accounts, a very talkative boy who loved nothing better than to accompany his father on one of his regular strolls around the neighborhood to chat with friends or colleagues. Diego rarely attended church because of his father's distrust of the Catholic leadership, even though his mother and her sisters were regular churchgoers. Diego later claimed that during one rare childhood visit to mass with an aunt, he was so bewildered by the praying around him that he ran to the front of the church and yelled at the worshippers for behaving in a way that he viewed as silly and ignorant. The artist's habit of making up stories about himself leads some scholars to doubt whether this incident ever really took place. These same historians suggest, however, that the kinds of falsehoods Diego told about himself provide important insights into his personality. For instance, his stories shed light on his life-long admiration for mythology and individual independence. "If Diego rarely told the simple truth, he did not tell simple lies either,"[12] said one biographer.

Memories of Drawing

"The earliest memory I have is that I was drawing."

Diego Rivera, *My Art, My Life*. New York: Dover, 1991, p. 9.

Throughout his childhood Diego's favorite activity was drawing.

> Almost as soon as my fat baby fingers could grasp a pencil, I was marking up walls, doors, and furniture. To avoid mutilation of his entire house, my father set aside a special room where I was allowed to write on anything I wished. This first 'studio' of mine had black canvas draped on all the walls and on the floor. Here I made my earliest 'murals.'[13]

Young Diego's favorite subjects for his drawings were machines and battle scenes. "I refused for a long time to draw mountains, owing to the fact that although Guanajuato was surrounded by them, I didn't know what was inside them,"[14] he acknowledged. One day, however, his father took him deep inside one of the silver mines that were cut into the nearby mountains. After the youngster emerged from this tour, mountains became one of his favorite subjects to draw.

Diego's first forays into drawing and art occurred at the same time that his father's standing in the Guanajuato community began to decline. Up to this point, Rivera Sr.'s status as a *criollo* and an army veteran who helped drive out the French had given him a measure of freedom to speak out against the policies of the Díaz regime. By the early 1890s, though, his pleas for democratic reforms were being met by the wider community with silence or outright hostility. During this same period, he decided to invest much of the family's savings in area silver mining operations. When these mines failed, Rivera fell into debt. He struggled with financial problems for the rest of his life.

In 1892, Diego's mother became so upset by these developments that she uprooted her family and left Guanajuato in one dramatic move. She waited until her husband departed for a work trip to the countryside, then sold virtually all of the family's furniture and other belongings. She then headed to Mexico City, the capital of

One of Rivera's cubist pieces titled Young Man with a Pen.

Mexico, with her five-year-old son and baby daughter in tow. Diego Sr. was stunned when he returned home to find his family gone. After weighing his options, though, he decided that he had no other choice but to follow his wife and children to Mexico City.

Life in Mexico City

The Rivera family struggled to adjust to their new surroundings. In the 1890s Mexico City contained about 400,000 residents, including a large number of foreign business executives and managers attracted by the business-friendly Porfiriato. Some parts of the city were scenic and vibrant. It included broad boulevards lined with electric lights, fancy restaurants, and theatres. Many of these establishments had a distinctly European feel to them, for many Mexicans continued to admire France and other European nations for their affluence and culture even after French forces had been chased out of Mexico in 1867. The city also featured bustling railroad terminals, newspaper offices, and telegraph stations that connected residents to the wider world.

During their first months in the capital, though, the Rivera family could not afford to sample any of the city's finer restaurants and theatres. The comforts of their previous middle-class existence were gone. Instead, like the majority of the city's residents, Diego and his family were forced to take up residence in a neighborhood that did not have running water, electricity, or indoor plumbing. Crime and disease were widespread in these communities, and the Rivera family soon fell victim to various illnesses. Diego spent long periods of time in bed battling scarlet fever, diphtheria, and typhoid. His mother became pregnant again, but her infant son Alfonso died after only one week of life.

Over time, though, the family's financial circumstances improved. Diego's mother managed to find regular work as a midwife, which enabled the family to move into a better neighborhood. The family received an additional financial boost in 1898, when Rivera Sr., who had been toiling as a restaurant cashier, secured a job as a clerk in the city's Department of Public Health.

Rivera painted this cubist piece titled Still Life with Cigar *in 1915. He experimented with several different art forms during his lifetime.*

First Years of School

Diego did not attend school for the first two years that his family lived in Mexico City. But he did receive valuable home schooling during this time. His parents tutored him and provided him with books, paper, and pencils to pursue his interests in reading and drawing. Diego's great-aunt, Vicenta, first introduced him to Mexican folk art at this time. The artists who made these engravings, paintings, and sculptures drew on Mexican history and culture for inspiration. Young Diego did not always understand the meaning or symbolism of some of these works, but he recognized the Mexican faces, professions, and settings featured in these paintings and engraving. These celebrations of Mexican heritage and life made a lasting impression on him.

In 1894 eight-year-old Diego was enrolled in school for the first time, but he lasted only three months at Colegio del Padre Antonio, a Catholic elementary school. He complained so bitterly about the school and its discipline-minded teachers that his mother finally withdrew him. The following year she enrolled her son at another Catholic school, Colegio Católico Carpantier. Diego performed well enough in his studies, but his teachers criticized his sloppy appearance and his spoiled attitude. They expressed particular unhappiness with his habit of skipping school to go play at nearby parks.

Several months later, Diego switched schools once again. At Liceo Católico Hispano-Mexicano, he finally found a school that seemed to suit him. "I was given good food as well as free instruction, books, various working tools, and other things," he recalled. "I was put in the third grade, but having been prepared well by my father, I was soon skipped to the sixth grade."[15]

A Young Art Prodigy

By the age of nine, young Diego was so passionate about drawing that he was certain that he would grow up to be an artist. His parents were delighted by his talent and enthusiasm, even though his drawings occasionally upset them. On one occasion, for example, the nine-year-old "executed a pencil sketch of his mother that was so unflatteringly accurate that she told him never to draw her again."[16]

By the time he was ten years old, Diego was constantly badgering his mother to enroll him in art class. She responded by registering him in evening classes at the prestigious San Carlos Academy of Fine Arts. Normally, a boy of Diego's age would not have been admitted into the academy, but his size (he was taller and heavier than most boys two or three years his senior) and talent convinced the school's administrators to allow him to attend.

Diego spent the next two years attending regular school by day and art classes at San Carlos in the evening. In 1898 he transferred to San Carlos full time. He spent the next seven years at the school, which had produced generations of well-known Mexican painters, engravers, and architects. Classes at San Carlos, however, emphasized European traditions and philosophies of art and paid less attention to native Mexican art. This state of affairs remained unchanged throughout Diego's years at the school, even though "the most vigorous art of the era was being made by less privileged Mexican artists: those who created cartoons, political engravings, and every variety of folk art."[17]

An Unusual Classmate

From his first days at San Carlos, Diego's appearance set him apart from his classmates. He remained a sloppy and careless dresser. One fellow student recalled how

> Rivera came to school in short pants and shocking-pink socks, his pockets stuffed with fearful boyish things—bent pins, odd bits of string, and earthworms that wriggled freely minus the luxury of a container. Between classes, and presumably more often, the fat boy would sneak out through back streets . . . and, sitting on the bank of the canal, feet dangling close to the stinking waters, fish.[18]

Diego's large, bulging eyes and heaviness also made him self-conscious at times. These feelings, combined with his ever-present curiosity and thirst for exploration, prompted many of his afternoon excursions outside the academy's walls. When he did not go fishing, he often wandered the markets of the city, soaking in the energy and color all around him. "The profusion of fruits and vegetables, the stalls abundant with flowers, the brightly colored peasant serapes and rebozos, gorgeously embroidered skirts and blouses, were a feast to the eye," wrote one biographer. "So were the murals painted on the walls of pulquerias, the bars where the fermented cactus drink called pulque was served."[19]

Back at the academy, Diego's work did not attract particular attention from classmates or instructors during his first few years. The teachers focused on mechanical skills and subjects such as geometry, architecture, and anatomy, so the young drawer did not have that many opportunities to show his creativity.

Eventually, however, a respected teacher named Santiago Rebull became intrigued by young Diego's work. Diego recalled their encounter in his autobiography:

> One day, when a class of about fifty students was painting a model, he singled me out. He found fault with my drawing, but he said, 'Just the same, what you're doing interests me. First thing tomorrow morning, come to my studio.' The other students flocked around to see what had interested old Rebull enough to extract an invitation to his studio, to which he had admitted no student for twenty years. They could see nothing and ascribed his enthusiasm to a senile whim. . . . But the next day the old man told me what he had discovered in my work was an interest in life and movement. Such an interest, he said, is the work of a genuine artist. 'These objects we call paintings,' he went on, 'are attempts to transcribe to a plane surface essential movements of life. A picture should contain the possibility of perpetual motion.' Rebull made me more aware than I had yet been of the laws of proportion and harmony, within which movement proceeds, and which are to be discerned in the masterpieces of all ages.[20]

Mentors and Inspirations

Two other San Carlos instructors also were important to young Diego's artistic development. One was Félix Parra, who passed his passion for native Mexican art forms and history on to the impressionable young artist. The other was José María Velasco, one of the giants of nineteenth-century Mexican art. A famous painter of portraits and Mexican landscapes, Velasco convinced young Diego that artists need to bring commitment and passion to their work if they are to have any hope of being successful or happy. In addition, his paintings profoundly influenced young Diego's ideas about composition and structure. In particular, Diego was struck by Velasco's dedication to realistic detail and his ability to convey the majesty of natural landscapes. "Velasco's

The Life of Posada

Underappreciated for much of his life, engraver and illustrator José Guadalupe Posada is now regarded as one of the most insightful and influential Mexican artists of the nineteenth and early twentieth centuries. Born in Augascalientes on February 2, 1852,

he first worked as a lithographer for various newspapers and book publishers. In 1888, he established his own print shop in Mexico City, and from this modest storefront he generated a huge number of broadsheets and other publications that took satiric aim at various aspects of Mexican society. He became particularly well-known during these years for his use of animated skeletons or *Calaveras* in his engravings and illustrations.

Posada's notoriety did not translate into riches, however, and when he died on January 20, 1913, he was a poor man. After his death, artists such as Diego Rivera and José Clemente Orozco credited Posada as a major influence on their own work.

An engraving titled El Gran Paneon *created by the underappreciated José Guadalupe Posada.*

art work is greater than a mural painting and a pyramid," Rivera later declared in his autobiography. "It is a poem of color with mountains as its stanzas."[21]

Years after leaving San Carlos, Rivera claimed that he also served as an unofficial apprentice to José Guadalupe Posada, a famous illustrator and engraver whose studio was only a few blocks from the academy. The subjects of Posada's engravings, which were printed on cheap paper and sold throughout the city for a few cents a piece, ranged from notorious crimes and political scandals to portraits of everyday scenes of Mexico City and its people. He was perhaps best known for his use of Calaveras, animated skeletons that Posada used to satirize and mock Mexican society. In the hands of Posada, the *Calaveras* became a sort of "x-ray of the collective soul of the people"[22] of Mexico.

Lessons From Posada

"[José Guadalupe Posada taught me that] the soul of every masterpiece is powerful emotion."

Diego Rivera, *My Art, My Life*. New York: Dover, 1991, p. 18.

Scholars today, however, debate whether Rivera ever even met Posada during his youth. Many biographers are skeptical of Rivera's apprenticeship claims, partly because there is no other evidence that the two artists had any relationship during his youth, and partly because of Diego's adult reputation as a liar.

Even if, as a teenager, he did not meet Posada, the engraver's work undoubtedly influenced Rivera later in his career. More than four decades after leaving San Carlos Academy, Rivera paid tribute to Posada by including him—arm in arm with "Calavera Catrina," one of the engraver's famous animated skeletons—in the center of his mural *Dream of a Sunday Afternoon in Alameda Park* (1947-1948).

Looking to Europe

During his late teens Diego became increasingly restless and impatient to begin the next phase of his artistic development.

As a result, he spent less and less time in the classrooms at San Carlos. Diego instead spent long days roaming the villages and fields outside of the capital. Here he found plenty of new and interesting subjects to paint and draw, from the faces of hard-working Indian peasants to the mountains surrounding Mexico City.

Diego also gained a greater understanding of social conditions in Mexico City around this time, as Rivera biographer Peter Hamill noted:

> In Mexico City, there were brutal divisions between the classes. The police of Don Porfirio [President Porfirio Díaz] penned the poor into wretched ghettos, where murder was a casual affair, health precarious, education nonexistent. On one street, Diego might see men in bowler hats and women wearing bustles and feathered boas; on another, he could witness the police battering a man into unconsciousness for the crime of walking barefoot into a 'good' neighborhood. Memories of this era would accompany him for the rest of his life and inform some of the best and worst of his art.[23]

These experiences fed Diego's growing obsession with the idea of continuing his artistic education in Europe. He wanted to study the great European artworks of history firsthand, learn from Europe's great teachers, and discuss art and life and politics with other young artists who made pilgrimages to Europe each year.

To this end, Diego managed to arrange a showing of some of his work to Teodoro A. Dehesa, the governor of the Mexican state of Veracruz. A well-known supporter of young Mexican artists, Dehesa was impressed with Diego's drawings and sympathetic to his desire to see the world beyond Mexico. He offered him a scholarship to study in Europe (about three hundred pesos a month), but told him that he would have to find the money for the voyage himself. Thrilled by this gesture of faith, Diego organized an exhibit of his paintings back in Mexico City in 1906. The exhibition was a success, and by the time it ended, he had sold enough of his drawings and paintings to pay for his passage to Europe.

Chapter 2

Learning From the Masters

Diego Rivera's artistic development was greatly influenced by the years he spent in Europe as a young man. He took classes from established artists, toured great museums, and spent endless hours debating issues of art, politics, and life with other young artists. During this time he explored the artistic movement known as Cubism and became fascinated by the mural work of Michelangelo and other ancient masters.

Dazzled by Europe

Rivera landed in Spain on January 6, 1907. Years later, Rivera recalled his youthful excitement upon arrival. "I remember, as if I saw it from another point in space, outside myself, a dimwit of twenty, so vain, so full of the blackheads of youth and dreams of being master of the universe, just like all the other fools of the age."[24]

Eager to soak in all of Spain's history and artistic tradition, Rivera settled in an apartment in Madrid and began studying with realist painter Eduardo Chicharro y Augera. He also spent long hours strolling the halls of the city's famed Prado Museum, where

Diego Rivera painted this piece titled Self-Portrait *in 1907.*

the works of influential artists such as Francisco de Goya (1746-1828), El Greco (1541-1614), Pieter Brueghel (c.1525-1569), and Hieronymus Bosch (c.1450-1516) were prominently displayed.

During his first weeks in Madrid, the young Mexican artist was shy and uncertain. As he became more comfortable in his new surroundings, though, he became a regular visitor to Madrid's bustling cafes. Fellow café patrons were initially unsure what to make of this big, heavy artist with the bulging eyes, sombrero-like hat, and wrinkled, paint-stained clothing. With each passing evening, however, Rivera's obvious intelligence and sense of humor became more evident. Within a matter of weeks, his arrival at the neighborhood cafés was greeted with shouts of welcome.

Rivera went out of his way to spend time with some of Madrid's older artists and writers. He particularly enjoyed the company of Spanish novelist Ramón del Valle-Inclán, an outgoing writer who had lost his left arm in a street fight during his youth. "[Valle-Inclán] was famous among his acquaintances for the fantastic versions he created of this event: Rivera evidently admired this gift for fabulous lies and he made it part of his own mature character."[25]

Moving On to Paris

During his time in Madrid, Rivera sent many paintings back to the governor of Veracruz, Teodoro A. Dehesa, his financial sponsor back in Mexico. Even though Dehesa praised the works, Rivera expressed frustration with the quality of these works. He explored different artistic styles in marathon sessions of painting, pushing his way through bouts of sickness and periods of great self-doubt. Yet despite all his efforts, he felt like he was making little progress in finding his own personal artistic vision. "I did very little painting of any worth during my year and a half in Spain,"[26] he wrote years later.

In the summer of 1909, Valle-Inclán convinced his frustrated young friend to leave Madrid for Paris, France, the center of the European art world. Rivera promptly fell in love with Paris. He spent his days painting canvas after canvas in city art academies, and then roamed the Paris cafés at night seeking out conversation and female company. Rivera's thirst for knowledge and inspiration also led him to travel to other major museums across Western Europe during this period.

It was in Paris, however, that Rivera's mind came most alive. He was fascinated by the work of famous French artists like Pablo Picasso (1881-1973) and Paul Cézanne (1839-1906), who had died the year before Rivera's arrival in Europe. He also devoured literature like never before. The works of German political philosopher Karl Marx made a particularly strong impression on the young artist. Marx championed a kind of socialism that became known as communism. He argued that all around the world, working people—farmers, factory workers, and other laborers—were being taken advantage of by the wealthy ruling elites that controlled most societies. Marx believed that destructive clashes between these two groups were inevitable, and he asserted that the only way to ensure social justice for all members of society was to divide wealth and power equally among all citizens. These arguments resonated with Rivera, who well remembered the desperation and anger of the poor and working-class people back in his native Mexico.

The Life of Paul Cézanne

The French painter Paul Cézanne was born on January 19, 1839, in Aix-en-Provence in southern France. For much of his life, critics and fellow painters dismissed and discounted his art. But his intensely personal vision of art, which challenged many traditional foundations of nineteenth-century European art, eventually became tremendously influential. It was a cornerstone of the cubist movement that brought Diego Rivera his first international attention. In addition, Cézanne's innovative approach to composition and color influenced the work of Pablo Picasso and other giants of twentieth-century art. Picasso even described Cézanne as "my one and only master" and "the father of us all." Cézanne died in his hometown on October 22, 1906, only a few years after his importance had finally begun to be recognized. Today, he is often described as the father of modern painting.

Self-Portrait, *by Paul Cézanne, who is often described as the father of modern painting.*

Rivera in London

In late 1909, Rivera's intellectual restlessness prompted him to make a month-long trip to London, England. His companions on this journey were María Gutierrez Blanchard, a painter who had been left hunchbacked by a childhood accident, and Angeline Beloff, a Russian artist. Beloff and Rivera had first met several months earlier. At first, the pretty young Russian painter viewed Rivera as a tiresome and overbearing man. The language barrier between the two artists also made it difficult for them to connect. During their visit to London, though, Rivera and Beloff became romantically involved.

The visit to London also deepened Rivera's belief in Marx's socialist vision. As he and his friends walked the streets of the city, they were stunned by the terrible poverty around them. He noticed that the factories of London were generating huge amounts of wealth for the owners, but that none of this wealth was trickling down to the laborers who sweated the hours away in dank and dangerous conditions.

Rivera spent most of the spring and summer of 1910 in France, where he produced a large number of paintings. Rivera sent many of these works back to Mexico, where they were warmly received. Rivera was heartened by his growing reputation there, and he began to weigh the possibility of paying a visit to his homeland.

Looking To Home

Rivera's mild interest in returning to Mexico became a priority when he learned that Mexican ruler Porfirio Díaz was planning a nationwide centennial celebration of Mexico's independence from Spain for the fall of 1910. Díaz decided that this grand celebration, which would include a month of parades, musical extravaganzas, lavish parties, and art exhibitions, would also be the perfect way to mark the thirtieth anniversary of his own reign.

Rivera was determined to participate in the huge celebration that was being planned back home. "In Paris, Diego Rivera was not yet a figure of stature in the world of art," explained one biographer. "In Mexico, he was somebody . . . and he wanted to be a part of it all."[27]

With this in mind, he contacted his sponsor, Governor Dehesa, and various government officials to let them know of his desires. He was subsequently invited to exhibit a selection of his paintings at a major centennial show being planned for San Carlos Academy, his alma mater, in late November.

Rivera took forty paintings with him on the long voyage to Veracruz. When he landed on October 2, he promptly transferred himself and his paintings to a train that was bound for Mexico City. After his arrival at the exhibit hall, Rivera spent long hours fussing over the presentation and arrangement of his paintings, which were to be shown in a solo exhibition. He then made the rounds of the cafés that he had frequented as a student. At each of these stops, he learned more about political storm clouds that had been gathering on Mexico's horizon over the previous months. Like many of his countrymen, Rivera began to wonder if the Díaz regime was about to be toppled.

Rivera, the Retriever

"In 1910 [Rivera] was a fledgling academic master, a docile retriever bringing back from Europe the artistic booty that his aged protector . . . had paid him to fetch."

Jean Charlot, *The Mexican Mural Renaissance, 1920-1925*. New Haven, CT: Yale University Press, 1962.

Turmoil in Mexico

During Rivera's years of study in Europe, a political opponent of Díaz, named Francisco Indalecio Madero, had emerged as a genuine threat to the dictator. Madero's increasing popularity triggered a wave of intimidation and violence from government forces, which escalated tensions across the country. Anxiety about the future of the country deepened on May 4, when Halley's Comet streaked over the skies of Mexico. To many Mexicans, the appearance of the comet was a sure omen of future death and disaster. One month later, Madero and thousands of his followers were arrested and imprisoned on trumped-up charges of plotting against the government. Then, in early July, Díaz was elected to yet another presidential term. Díaz and his allies claimed that his re-election provided clear evidence of his enduring popularity, but ordinary Mexicans knew the truth: they were living in a police state with no real political choices.

The 1910 elections proved to be the final straw for many of Mexico's long-suffering people. By the time the San Carlos art show was ready to open its doors, rebels fighting under the banner of the Mexican Liberal Party (PLM) had captured large sections of Mexico's northern states from government forces. Other northern rebels loyal to Madero were led by the dashing Francisco "Pancho" Villa and Álvaro Obregón. In the southern states, meanwhile, many poor Mexicans rushed to the side of Emiliano Zapata, yet another revolutionary who vowed to give Mexican peasants a greater share of the nation's land and wealth.

Throughout the first weeks of November, Mexico City's cafés and neighborhoods swirled with rumors and reports about the latest movements and battles in the countryside. Rivera listened with interest, but his primary focus remained on his upcoming exhibition at San Carlos. The show, which opened on November 20, was a great success. Díaz's wife bought six of his paintings, and other wealthy patrons snapped up most of Rivera's other works. Weary but delighted, Rivera then booked passage on a ship for Europe.

By the end of the exhibition, Rivera had clearly established himself as one of Mexico's premier young artists. But his priorities during these late months of 1910—the opening months of the decade-long Mexican Revolution, which tossed the country into chaos and claimed an estimated one million lives—came back to haunt him years later, when he had positioned himself as a champion of the peasantry and working-class. During the centennial celebrations in Mexico City, he had decided that his top priority was to rub shoulders with wealthy art patrons in order to advance his career. At the same time, thousands of his countrymen were simultaneously deciding to put their lives at risk in the pursuit of greater social justice. Rivera later insisted that he had been an active supporter of the Revolution during these pivotal opening months. He even claimed that he had been forced to leave Mexico or be killed by agents of the regime. Historians have determined, however, that all of these claims were falsehoods.

Return to Europe

When Rivera returned to Paris in early 1911, he left his celebrity status behind in Mexico. "Measured against artistic developments in Paris, [Rivera was] a conservative and marginal artist"[28] at this time. Still, the painter returned to Europe with renewed confidence and energy.

Rivera and Cubism

"It should [not] be surprising that Rivera abandoned Cubism. In reality he had never felt comfortable with it. It must have seemed too narrow, a small corner of a vast field that had begun to open before him."

Jorge Hernández Campos, "The Influence of the Classical Tradition, Cézanne, and Cubism on Rivera's Artistic Development." In *Diego Rivera*, edited by Linda Downs and Detroit Institute of Arts. New York: W.W. Norton, 1986, p. 122.

Rivera's return to Paris also enabled him to reunite with Angeline Beloff, who had missed him terribly during his absence. "Our reunion was rapturous," Rivera later said. "We now decided to live together."[29] According to Beloff's memoirs, she and Rivera married a short time after his return, in June 1911. No official records have been found to confirm this claim, but historians regard Beloff's memoirs as reliable in most other respects. In addition, Rivera often referred to her as his common-law wife over the next several years.

Back in Mexico, meanwhile, Francisco Madero and his followers had succeeded in overthrowing Díaz and forcing him into exile in May 1911. Madero was elected president of Mexico a few months later. Rivera was delighted by this turn of events, and his happiness increased when the newly installed Madero government awarded him a study grant.

Rivera's optimism about Mexico's new president faded quickly, however. As the months passed, Rivera waited in vain for word of land reforms or other policy changes that would help the poor and landless peoples of his homeland. Rivera's sadness deepened when he learned that Madero did not intend to pursue major land redistribution policies—a decision that turned Zapata and many of his former followers against the president.

In February 1913, Rivera was nonetheless shocked to hear that Madero had been assassinated by General Victoriano Huerta, a murder that "triggered the bloodiest, most prolonged stage of the Mexican Revolution, essentially a countrywide civil war."[30] Madero's assassination also ended the flow of grant money from the Mexican government into Rivera's pocket.

Exploring Cubism

As Madero's last months in office were ticking away, Rivera continued to soak in the glamour and intellectual diversity of Paris. He and Beloff set up house in a neighborhood heavily sprinkled with writers, professors, sculptors, and painters. One of these artists was the young Italian painter and sculptor Amedeo Modigliani, who loved doing sketches of Rivera's fleshy features. Years later, Modigliani would become famous, but during these years in Paris he was an alcoholic and drug addict. Another friend and influence during this period was Mexican painter Best Maugard, who spent several weeks traveling through Spain with Rivera in 1912.

Rivera's canvases, meanwhile, reflected his continued search for a style that suited and inspired him. "Dissatisfied as ever, he swung rapidly from one painting style to another, passionately defending whatever style he was enamored with at the time, only to denounce it later."[31] When exhaustion or frustration overtook him, Rivera often retreated to the familiar comfort of the city's many cafés. He often stayed out all night, sharing stories and debating politics with fellow artists and intellectuals.

In 1913, Rivera finally decided to dedicate his talents to cubism, an art form that had exploded in popularity across Europe over the previous few years due to the work of such famous artists as Picasso, Cézanne, Georges Braque (1882-1963), and Piet Mondrian (1872-1944). In the cubist form, painters break subjects down into their essential geometric forms, such as cylinders, squares, spheres, and pyramids. The resulting pictures often look like a broken, jumbled version of the subject. Most of the early trailblazers in this art form painted in somber earth tones.

Rivera's 1913 painting *Girl with Artichokes* marked his first effort to clearly incorporate the ideas of cubism. From that point forward, he generated an enormous number of cubist paintings—more than two hundred over the course of the next four years. During that time, he became one of the movement's leading innovators. "Rivera developed his own bold cubist style," observed one biographer. "[Rivera dipped] his brush into bright tropical colors instead of the grays of the other cubists, creating what became known as decorative or synthetic cubism."[32] Rivera was able to indulge his newfound passion for cubism because of the supportive efforts of Beloff, who painted and sold reproductions of European master-works to buy food for their table and pay their rent.

Paintings like Pablo Picasso's Friendship I, *inspired Rivera's work as a cubist.*

Rivera and Picasso

Early in Rivera's cubist period, he built a short-lived but intense friendship with the temperamental Picasso. Writing in his auto-biography, Rivera recalled his first visit to the famous artist's studio. "Picasso's studio was full of his exciting canvases," he wrote. "Grouped together they had an impact more powerful than when shown by dealers as individual masterpieces. They were like living parts of an organic world Picasso had himself created."[33]

Picasso was so impressed by the artistic promise of his young Mexican friend that he helped arrange Rivera's first one-man exhi-bition in Paris in April 1914, at the city's prestigious Galerie Weill. "Being accepted by the master of Cubism himself was, of course, a source of tremendous personal satisfaction to me," Rivera said. "Not only did I consider Picasso a great artist, but I respected his critical judgment, which was severe and keen."[34]

After the show, Rivera and Beloff and several friends went on an extended tour of Spain. During this trip they learned that Archduke Francis Ferdinand of Austria had been assassinated on June 28, 1914. This murder triggered a complex series of events that resulted in World War I, a four-year conflict that devastated much of Europe. When Rivera and Beloff returned to Paris in 1915, they found a city that had been transformed by war. Citywide curfews had been imposed, and citizens went to bed every night fearing German bombers would wake them from their sleep. Rivera was also despondent to discover that many of his artist friends had gone off to fight in the war.

Triumph and Despair

In 1915, Rivera finished *Zapatista Landscape—The Guerrilla*, which art critics view as his cubist masterpiece. This work, which features a Mexican sombrero, a rifle, a wooden box, and scraps of native Indian fabric set against a backdrop of moun-tains, had been inspired by reports from Mexico that Zapata and Villa had occupied Mexico City. Rivera later called it "probably the most faithful expression of the Mexican mood that I have ever achieved."[35]

Art critics view Zapatista Landscape—The Guerilla *as Rivera's cubist masterpiece.*

During this period, though, Rivera's affiliation with Picasso and his growing reputation combined to make the artist even more self-centered. Though he possessed undeniable charisma, some of his remaining artist friends grew weary of his constant lying and apparent need to always be the center of attention. Other artists continued to flock to his side, however. One of these was a beautiful Russian painter named Marevna Vorobieva-Stebelska, who soon became Rivera's mistress.

On August 11, 1916, Beloff gave birth to a son, Diego Jr. Wartime shortages of basic goods made it difficult for her and Rivera to keep the baby warm and well-fed. The pressure of caring for a newborn was further intensified by Rivera's ambivalent attitude toward the baby. On the one hand, he was proud and happy to have a son. Yet he also resented the baby's demands on their time and the inevitable interruptions that the baby made to his work schedule. "If the baby cried or shouted while he worked, he would be capable—he said—of throwing the baby out the window,"[36] recalled Beloff.

A few months after Diego Jr. was born, Rivera abruptly ended his relationship with Beloff. He announced that he wanted to be with Vorobieva, who he found to be "terribly exciting."[37] Hurt and depressed, Beloff moved out of their apartment. She spent the next several months struggling to care for the baby herself, with virtually no help from Rivera.

Rivera then returned to Beloff's side as suddenly as he had left it. Explaining that life with Vorobieva was exhausting, he asked Beloff to take him back. Beloff still loved Rivera, so she set aside her feelings of betrayal and moved back in to their apartment. A few weeks later, however, she reluctantly sent the baby to live with relatives in a Paris suburb. The infant was returned to them several months later, but the reunion was short-lived. Diego Jr. died in the great influenza epidemic of 1918, which claimed millions of lives around the world.

Revolution in Russia

Despite the chaos in Rivera's personal life during this time, he followed the events of World War I with great interest. The year 1917 was a particularly momentous one in the war. France struggled with wide-scale mutinies within its military ranks, and the United States entered the war against Germany. The news that most excited Rivera, however, came from Russia. Widespread anger and despair over the war's toll on Russia's young men finally brought public dissatisfaction with Czar Nicholas II to the boiling point. Led by Russian revolutionaries Vladimir Lenin and Leon Trotsky, Russian peasants and workers rose up against their government. By the end of the year, this socialist movement—which promised to withdraw Russia from World War I, redistribute land to millions of peasants, and hand control of industry over to workers—had taken charge of the vast nation.

On March 3, 1918, Russia signed a separate peace treaty with Germany. The end of hostilities on the eastern front aided Germany's cause, but over the next several months it became clear that Germany would not be able to overcome the entrance of the United States into the war. On November 11, 1918, Germany reluctantly signed a peace agreement that forced the nation to dismantle its military completely.

The success of the 1917 October Revolution led Rivera, Beloff, and some of their Russian friends to discuss the possibility of traveling to the new Soviet Union. They dreamed of documenting the changes taking place in Moscow and other Russian cities on canvas. But when Rivera and Modigliani applied for visas, their applications were denied.

The Russian Revolution also led Rivera to question whether cubism was an effective way to reach the hearts and minds of ordinary people. He expressed growing doubts about the value of cubism as a vehicle for commenting on the history and nobility of farmers and other working people, whether they lived in Russia or Mexico or somewhere else. "When it dawned on me that all this innovation [in artistic style] had little to do with real life, I would surrender all the glory and acclaim cubism had brought me for a way in art truer to my inmost feelings,"[38] he later wrote.

Turning away from Cubism

In 1918, Rivera abandoned cubism and returned to painting works that were grounded in realism. Rivera later claimed that:

> I stopped painting in the cubist manner because of the war, the Russian Revolution, and my belief in the need for a popular and socialized art. It had to be a functional art, related to the world and to the times, and had to serve to help the masses to a better social organization.[39]

Another factor in Rivera's withdrawal from cubism may have been his increasingly strained relationship with Picasso. By the late 1910s, Rivera felt that he needed to assert his independence from his Spanish mentor—and his own Mexican identity. Picasso's habit of swiping artistic ideas and methods for his own use was also beginning to irritate Rivera.

Pining for Mexico

Rivera's decision to return to realism baffled and angered some of his artist friends, who had flooded back into Paris after the war ended. The painter fell into a series of well-publicized spats with friends and colleagues, including influential art dealer Léonce Rosenberg. Rivera's relationship with Beloff continued to deteriorate as well, especially after the death of their son in late 1918. By early 1919, Rivera found himself unwelcome in many parts of the French art community.

As a result of all these factors, Rivera was an unhappy and restless painter when he met his countryman and fellow painter David Alfaro Siqueiros in early 1919. The two artists spent the next several months in each other's company, debating about art and politics late into the night. Meanwhile, Beloff toiled away thanklessly on her art reproductions so that she could put food on their table.

Rivera closely followed the Mexican Revolution with fellow countryman and painter David Alfaro Siqueiros.

Rivera and Siqueiros followed the twists and turns of the ongoing Mexican Revolution with great interest. When they heard that Zapata had been assassinated by agents of President Venustiano Carranza in April 1919, the two Mexican artists decided that "a truly Mexican art must be created to help advance the Revolution's original goals of land for the landless, workers' rights, genuine popular democracy, and national ownership of natural resources."[40]

The Call of Home

In the early 1920s, Mexico's political environment changed in ways that convinced Rivera to return home. In May 1920, Carranza was assassinated, and four months later, former revolutionary Álvaro Obregón was elected president. Obregón appointed education officials who wanted to support and invigorate Mexican arts. These administrators were especially interested in art that recognized the contributions of the Mexican working class and the history and traditions of native art forms.

A Legend of Mexican Art

David Alfaro Siqueiros, who ranks with Diego Rivera and José Clemente Orozco as one of the leading figures of the Mexican Renaissance art movement of the twentieth century, was born on December 29, 1896, in Chihuahua, Mexico. After fighting in the Mexican Revolution as a member of the Constitutionalist Army, he worked in Europe as a diplomat. Shortly after arriving in Europe, he became friends with Rivera and began his own education as an artist. A great supporter of the proletariat—the working class—he returned to Mexico in the early 1920s and began creating what he called "an art for all." For the next four decades, he divided his energies between political activism and the creation of great murals that glorified Mexico's pre-colonial past and revolutionary spirit. His most famous creation was *The March of Humanity on Earth and Toward the Cosmos*, a 50,000-square-foot mural that also featured architectural and sculptural elements. By the time of his death, on January 6, 1974, he was one of Mexico's most famous and beloved citizens.

*In 1920, Rivera spent several weeks studying the frescoes the
Michelangelo painted on the ceiling of the Sistine Chapel in Rome, Italy.*

As the climate in Mexico became more favorable to artists, Rivera
spent virtually all of 1920 in Italy studying Renaissance-era art. He
spent weeks studying Rome's Sistine Chapel, marveling at the massive frescoes that Michelangelo had painted on the ceiling. He found
himself drawn to other large-scale mural paintings as well. By the
time he returned to Paris in May 1921, Rivera knew that he wanted
to further explore the art form of the mural. "During that period [of
travel in Italy], he created more than three hundred drawings and
achieved the integration of intellectual power and artistic vision
with which he returned to Mexico,"[41] wrote one scholar.

In June 1921, Rivera set sail for Mexico. He promised Beloff that
he would send for her as soon as he got resettled and had enough
money. He never fulfilled this promise, however. In fact, they never
spoke to each other again. Years later, Rivera admitted that he treat-
ed his first wife terribly. "She gave me everything a good woman
can give to a man," he noted. "In return, she received from me all
the heartache and misery that a man can inflict upon a woman."[42]

Chapter 3

Inspiring Change in Mexico

During the 1920s, Diego Rivera increasingly focused on muralism, the artistic form for which he became best known. He continued to produce paintings on canvas in order to pay his bills and keep a roof over his head, but he directed most of his imagination and energies toward the brightly colored mural paintings he created on the walls of some of Mexico's best-known buildings. Many of these murals were loaded with political, cultural, and historical imagery designed to jolt the Mexican people into a new era of national pride. Numerous scholars believe that Rivera's efforts in this regard were successful. "Rivera's role in Mexico's rediscovery of its past and the roots of its culture cannot be overestimated,"[43] declared one art historian.

Rebirth in Mexico

When Rivera returned to Mexico from Europe in 1921, he claimed that the vibrant colors of the Mexican landscape and marketplace and the bustling energy of the farmers and shopkeepers immediately inspired him. At times he felt that every street corner and field contained a scene worth sketching. Working furiously, he filled entire notebooks with sketches of his countrymen and women. During these weeks, he felt his true artistic vision taking shape. Years later, he said that:

> my homecoming produced an aesthetic exhilaration which it is impossible to describe. It was as if I were being born anew, born in a new world. . . . My style was born as children are born, in a moment, except that this birth had come after a torturous pregnancy of 35 years.[44]

As Rivera roamed Mexico City and the surrounding countryside, he listened intently to news about an ambitious new public mural program that was being set in motion by José Vasconcelos, President Álvaro Obregón's new minister of education. Vasconcelos was a smart and idealistic man who wanted to lift all Mexicans to a higher level of education and enlightenment. Since most Mexicans could not read, Vasconcelos came to believe that public murals could be used to instill a greater appreciation of Mexican history and values in all Mexicans, whether they were *criollos* (people of Spanish or other European descent), indigenous Indians, or *mestizos* (people of mixed European and indigenous heritage).

During his first few months back in Mexico, Rivera noticed that some artists had already received government commissions to create public murals at various sites around the country. These artists had been given the freedom to paint about whatever subjects they chose, and they operated without any governmental deadlines. The working conditions enabled these artists to explore all sorts of themes and styles. Years later, this brief but exciting era in Mexican art became known as the "Mexican Renaissance."

Most of the murals created during this period were frescoes, which are mural paintings done on fresh wet plaster. As the paint and plaster dry together, the paint becomes permanently bound to the plaster. Rivera was eager to join the ranks of public muralists, but Vasconcelos expressed doubts about whether the celebrity painter could still produce "Mexican" art after his many years of study in Europe. "For the first six months [back in Mexico] I painted no frescoes but supported myself with a succession of bizarre jobs,"[45] Rivera recalled. The artist's unhappiness was further heightened by the death of his father from cancer in late 1921. By all accounts, the painter took the news of Rivera Sr.'s death very hard.

A Champion of Education

José Vasconcelos was a Mexican official who provided essential governmental support for mural painting across Mexico in the early 1920s. Without his vision and energy, the "Mexican Renaissance" that lifted Diego Rivera to international stardom might have never taken place. Born on February 28, 1882, in Oaxaca, Mexico, Vasconcelos was a lieutenant of revolutionary leader Francisco Madero, who helped topple dictator Porfirio Díaz in 1911. When Madero's government fell two years later, Vasconcelos went into exile.

Vasconcelos returned to Mexico in 1920, when Álvaro Obregón was elected president. He worked in the early 1920s as rector of the National University of Mexico and as Obregón's minister of education. Vasconcelos launched an ambitious scheme to increase literacy rates and public interest in education. As part of this latter goal, he developed a huge mural painting project. Rivera and other talented young artists seized this opportunity to use murals to teach Mexicans about their history. In 1924, however, political pressures forced Vasconcelos to end the program and submit his resignation. He went back into exile until 1929, when he made a failed bid for the presidency of Mexico. Vasconcelos died in Mexico City on June 30, 1959.

Without the vision and energy of José Vasconcelos the "Mexican Renaissance" may never have occurred.

Reassuring Vasconcelos

Rivera's fortunes changed in November 1921, when he took a trip with Vasconcelos to the Yucatán Peninsula in southeastern Mexico. Centuries ago, the ancient Mayan civilization had thrived in this region. Rivera was mesmerized by the surviving murals that adorned the ruins of that ancient world. By the end of the journey, Vasconcelos was convinced that he and Rivera shared the same basic vision of the public mural program.

Upon returning to Mexico City, Vasconcelos commissioned Rivera to paint a mural at the National Preparatory School in Mexico City. It was here that he completed his first monumental mural, a 1,000-square-foot account of the biblical story of Creation. This mural showed glimpses of the artist's later brilliance, but Rivera himself acknowledged later in life that the work was a flawed, cautious effort.

Around this same time Rivera met a striking young woman named Guadalupe "Lupe" Marín, and the two began a passionate love affair. They were married in 1922. Rivera also joined the Mexican Communist Party at the end of the year. This small but dedicated group was determined to advance the cause of communism across Mexico. In keeping with core Communist beliefs, party members called for equal ownership of all state resources and wealth among all members of society. Rivera became one of the group's leaders within a matter of months.

The Syndicate of Technical Workers, Painters, and Sculptors

In late 1922, Rivera helped found the Syndicate of Technical Workers, Painters, and Sculptors. These artists announced that syndicate members intended to create art not just for the ruling elites, but for everyone in Mexican society, including the oppressed poor and indigenous people of the nation. In terms of its political orientation, the Syndicate showed a strong Communist influence. Rivera was elected president of the union in 1923. He enjoyed the prestige of the post, in part because it gave him many opportunities to offer his opinions. As the months passed, though, it became clear that fellow muralist

David Alfaro Siqueiros, who was a tireless organizer and advocate, was the true heart of the union.

Rivera spent countless hours with Siqueiros and other Syndicate members during this period. The house that he shared with Marín became a central gathering place for artists, writers, and Communist activists throughout Mexico City. "Diego was older than most of them and, thanks to his years in Europe, more sophisticated," noted one biographer. "He assumed the role of mentor, ward boss, and master of revels. He was funny, smart, entertaining, worldly, and passionate about painting. Lupe was funny, smart, a great cook, and passionate about everything else."[46]

Rivera paid his bills in 1922 and 1923 with canvas paintings, but mural work remained his obsession. On many occasions, he infuriated his wife with his spending decisions. Instead of using his limited earnings to pay the rent or buy groceries, he sometimes spent the money on pre-Conquest sculptures (sculptures created by indigenous Mexican people before the arrival of Spanish con-

Rivera's fresco titled New World Schoolteacher *is one of several frescoes he completed between 1924 and 1928 on the Ministry of Education building in Mexico City.*

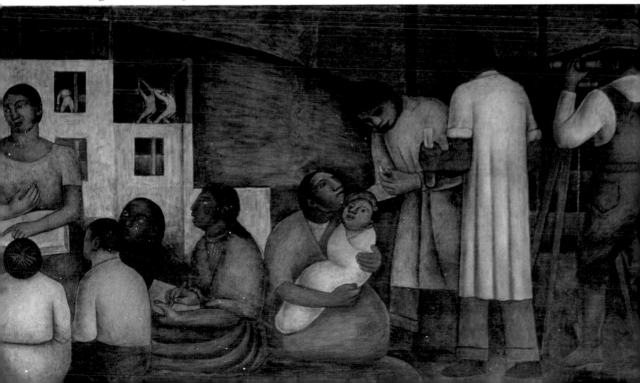

querors in the sixteenth century). On other occasions he made hefty donations to the Mexican Communist Party.

Journey to Tehauntepec

Despite the many demands on his time, Rivera still managed to continue his exploration of Mexico's historical and cultural past. In late 1922, for instance, he went on another trip sponsored by Vasconcelos. This time Rivera journeyed to the Isthmus of Tehauntepec, an area of Mexico where indigenous peoples had been left largely undisturbed over the centuries. Rivera was bowled over by the appearance of these villagers, who had the dark skin and broad features of their Indian ancestors. By the time he left the region, his fascination with traditional Mexican culture had become a virtual fever. "Rivera came back from Tehuantepec shaken into simplicity by all he had seen and experienced,"[47] recalled one colleague.

Rivera's memories of Tehuantepec were still fresh in March 1923, when he began a new mural project commissioned by Vasconcelos. This commission called on him to place murals on the interior walls of the massive Ministry of Education building in Mexico City. It was a huge job and Rivera maintained an exhausting pace. Surrounded by assistants who prepared the wall and paints for him, the artist routinely painted for fourteen or sixteen hours at a time. On at least one occasion he fell from the scaffolding on which he was standing in complete exhaustion. Another time, one of his assistants recalled how:

> late one of the first evenings that we were on the job, as I walked through the darkened court I noticed that the painter's scaffold was trembling as if at the start of an earthquake. Coming near, I saw Rivera's dim bulk at the top. Climbing up to investigate, I found him crying and viciously picking off his day's job with a small trowel as a child will kick down a sand castle in a tantrum.[48]

Rivera's progress on the Ministry of Education frescoes was further complicated by growing opposition to Vasconcelos's mural program. By this time, wealthy and influential members of Mexican society were outraged by some of the murals that were appearing across the country. These murals, many of which had been designed and painted by Syndicate artists with Communist leanings, often portrayed the nation's elite in a negative light. Conservative newspapers demanded an end to the mural program, and vandalism of some murals became common. When Vasconcelos's efforts to defuse the crisis failed, he stopped commissioning new murals and called a halt to virtually every mural project that was in progress. In 1924, under pressure, Vasconcelos resigned his post as the minister of education.

Rivera's Mexico

"Images from [Rivera's] Ministry of Education cycle continue to be used today as book jackets, album covers, and posters; they represent Mexico to the world, and in some ways, to Mexicans themselves."

Peter Hamill, *Diego Rivera*. New York: Abrams, 1999.

One Artist Left Standing

The attacks on the government mural program triggered a crisis within the Syndicate. Most union members were enraged by the decision to suspend the program. They vowed to broadcast their political and social commentary through other artistic means. Rivera, though, responded to the controversy by resigning from the union.

Most of the Syndicate membership, including long-time friends and colleagues such as Siqueiros, bitterly condemned Rivera for his decision. They claimed that he abandoned his fellow artists in a desperate bid to keep his work at the National Education building from being shut down. Rivera strongly denied this charge, but as it turned out he was the only muralist who kept his commission. All others were kicked out of the city's public spaces, and their half-finished works were abandoned or painted over.

Even as Rivera's professional isolation grew, his personal circumstances also underwent dramatic change. In 1924, Lupe Marín gave birth to a daughter, also named Lupe. Two years later, Marín and Rivera had a second daughter, Ruth. Rivera left most parenting duties to his wife. As she cared for their two small children, the painter virtually lived at the National Education building and in the lively cafés that dotted the surrounding streets. When Rivera did come home, it was usually to eat or bathe (he often went days at a time without washing, which greatly disgusted Marín). This thoughtless behavior, combined with rumors that the painter often sought out the company of other women, made Marín angry and resentful.

Triumph in Chapingo

Rivera spent little time worrying about Marín's feelings. His focused remained on his art. In the fall of 1924, Rivera took a break from his Ministry of Education work to paint a set of murals at the new National School of Agriculture in Chapingo, Mexico. Scholars agree that he never would have received this commission from the Obregón government if he had not resigned from the Syndicate earlier that year. He spent the next several months dividing his time between his two massive art projects.

Today, the murals Rivera painted at Chapingo are considered to be among the artist's crowning achievements. He painted a total of thirty-nine frescoes at the college, including a number of spectacular murals in the college's Spanish-style chapel. Years later, Rivera said that the unifying theme of the Chapingo murals was "the origins of the sciences and the arts, a kind of abbreviated version of the essential history of mankind."[49]

Many of the frescoes emphasized the links between Mexicans and the land on which they lived. Rivera included several female nudes meant to represent the glory and fertility of nature (Marín served as his primary model for these figures). He also included scenes depicting the natural cycle of life (such as seedlings sprouting into flowers) and implied that societies could undergo similar growth and change. For example, his Chapingo frescoes included scenes of poor peasants rebelling against wealthy landowners. The work also featured a politically charged painting of the body of revolutionary leader Emiliano Zapata, his blood soaking and fertilizing the soil around him. Years later, Rivera described the murals he painted at Chapingo as "a song of the land, its profundity, beauty, richness, and sadness."[50]

Conservative politicians, landowners, professors, and religious leaders grumbled about the symbolism in some of the Chapingo frescoes. They viewed Rivera's commentary on Mexico and its people as a potential threat to their comfortable place in Mexican society. By this time, however, Rivera's international stardom had become so great that they decided that shutting down his work would just bring more attention to his political beliefs.

Rivera hoped that the powerful images in the Chapingo murals would inspire Mexico's common people to join together and demand social and political change. He wanted them to gain a greater recognition of their importance to the country's past, present, and future. Through his work, he also suggested that embracing Communist ideals was the best way for Mexican people to obtain a better life for themselves and their families. In one Chapingo fresco, for example, Rivera includes a dashing figure who is pointing urgently at a hammer and sickle, which is the symbol of the Communist Soviet Union. The same figure is wearing a shirt of red, a color closely associated with communism. Rivera was unaware that at the same time that he was painting this tribute, thousands of Soviet peasants were being imprisoned and murdered by Soviet leader Joseph Stalin and his followers.

Chapingo Frescoes

Rivera's frescoes at Chapingo are notable because they "contain the salient [defining] characteristics of Rivera's style: a reliance on the linear language of drawing; two-dimensional composition; sensual forms; and a rich, sumptuous use of color."

Ida Rodríguez-Pramplini, "Rivera's Concept of History." In *Diego Rivera*, edited by Linda Downs and Detroit Institute of Arts. New York: W.W. Norton, 1986.

Visiting Russia

In 1927, Rivera was invited to Moscow to represent his nation's Communist Party at the tenth anniversary celebration of the Russian Revolution. The artist marveled at the huge parades that he witnessed to mark the occasion. He also visited with many painters, sculptors, and other artists during his travels around the country. Rivera's most notable encounter, however, was with Leon Trotsky. A key figure in the Russian Revolution, Trotsky was on the verge of being chased out of the country by the power-hungry Stalin. Despite the growing tension surrounding the revolutionary leader, Trotsky and Rivera managed to become friends.

After eight months in Russia, Rivera returned home to Mexico in June 1928 with dozens of drawings and paintings of Russian life in his bags. He told his friends and colleagues that his time in Moscow and other Russian cities had deepened his commitment to proletariat art—art for the working people. He mentioned nothing about the brutal methods that Stalin was using to maintain power across the young Soviet empire.

Rivera's silence about Stalin's campaign of violence and intimidation has sparked debate among historians and biographers. As one Rivera biographer asked, "Did he completely miss what was happening all around him in the Soviet Union? Was he blind? A fool? . . . How could Diego Rivera, whose public art argued passionately against oppression, have failed to see oppression in the Soviet Union?"[51] Some scholars now claim that he simply did not know or understand the situation. Others assert that his devotion to the abstract idea of communism blinded him to the growing nightmare in the Soviet Union. In any case, Rivera never really addressed this issue in any of his later writings or interviews.

Rivera's Mexico City Masterpiece

By the time Rivera returned to Mexico from Russia, his work at the Ministry of Education was nearly complete. He applied the final touches to several frescoes, then began preparing for the grand unveiling. In November 1928, four long years after he had begun painting his first fresco in the building, he presented his finished work to the world. It included 128 murals on three floors and covered 17,000 square feet of wall and ceiling space.

Rivera's murals at the education building are divided into two sections. The court of Labor presents Mexicans farming, mining,

The Author of the "Great Terror"

Joseph Stalin was one of the most infamously brutal and ruthless world leaders of the twentieth century. During his long dictatorship over the Soviet Union—and especially during a mid-1930s period known as the "Great Terror"—Stalin murdered or imprisoned millions of his own people in order to keep his iron grip on power.

Stalin was born as Josif Vissarionovich Dzhugashvili on December 18, 1879, in Gori, Georgia, then part of Russia. A fiery supporter of the 1917 Russian Revolution, he rose rapidly through the Communist Party ranks after Vladimir Lenin took power in Moscow. When Lenin died in 1924, Stalin moved quickly to take his place.

By the late 1920s, Stalin was firmly entrenched as the new leader of the Soviet Union. Over the next two decades, he invested a great deal of money to develop the nation's industrial and military strength. This investment proved vital in stopping Germany during World War II. But he also snuffed out millions of lives with his brutal policies. Many of these people were executed during Stalin's paranoid purges of the Communist Party. Others died after being herded onto massive state-run farms, where hunger, disease, and exhausting workdays were commonplace. During his final years of power, the Soviet Union became an atomic power and expanded its reach into much of Eastern Europe. Stalin died of a stroke on March, 5, 1953.

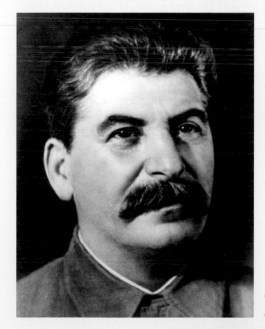

Communist dictator Joseph Stalin was one of the most brutal leaders of the twentieth century.

and working in factories, but it also intersperses these scenes with frescoes of Mexican art, dance, music, and poetry. The court of Fiesta, meanwhile, depicts popular festivals and folk ballads. All together, wrote one critic, "the murals in the Ministry of Education make up a visual ballad of Mexico, resembling the traditional corrido, a narrative in song."[52]

Other scholars have echoed these sentiments. As one of Rivera's biographers observed, future historians who studied these frescoes could easily "reconstruct a rich and varied picture of the Mexican land, its people, their labors, festivals, [and] ways of living."[53]

Rivera's frescoes also packed a significant political impact, especially when seen as a single body of work. Some panels signaled his support for the Communist cause, others condemned Mexico's elite ruling class, and still others pondered the future effect of technological progress on humanity. Taken together, these murals served as a call to action addressed to the nation's long-suffering poor and landless.

An Artist in Command

Rivera's work at the National Education building in the 1920s is still regarded as one of the high points of his career. "[It is] undoubtedly Rivera's greatest achievement as a muralist," wrote one art scholar. "It is in these murals where Rivera's fully formed style first appears, and where his aesthetic-political agenda comes together."[54] Another historian noted that "by the time of this mural, Rivera was in full command of the fresco technique, the palette brighter and lusher."[55]

Rivera recognized the importance of this work as well. "Mexican muralism—for the first time in the history of monumental painting—ceased to use gods, kings, chiefs of state, heroic generals, etc., as central heroes," he declared.

> For the first time in the history of art, Mexican mural painting made the masses the hero of monumental art. That is to say, the man of the fields, of the factories, of the cities, and towns. When a hero appears among the people, it is clearly as part of the people and as one of them.[56]

Part of the Ministry of Education mural, Rivera's Day of the Dead— City Fiesta *reconstructs the Mexican people's way of living and how they celebrated life.*

Trouble at Home

Rivera's rewarding work at the National Education building helped him forget the end of his stormy marriage to Marín. She had left him a year earlier, fed up with his selfish behavior and many affairs. Marín had been particularly infuriated by her husband's romantic involvement with Tina Modotti, a photographer who had modeled for him. Wracked with anger, she destroyed several of his paintings in retaliation and vowed to leave him for good.

Rivera took responsibility for the failure of the marriage. "The quarrels over [my] infidelities carried over into quarrels over everything else," he admitted. "Frightful scenes marked our life together."[57] He also found Marín impossible to live with, and he felt relieved when the marriage finally came to an end.

Rivera's bachelor status made it even easier for him to manage romantic liaisons with the many beautiful women who were drawn to his celebrity status and charismatic ways. He forgot many of these women within a matter of days. But then a young woman named Frida Kahlo entered his life and changed it forever.

Chapter 4

Creating Controversy in America

In 1929, Diego Rivera married fellow painter Frida Kahlo, and from that point forward the couple became the subject of worldwide fascination and gossip. Rivera painted murals in several major American cities that attracted both warm praise and angry criticism, but his turbulent personal life attracted nearly as much attention as his art.

Detective Rivera

The year 1929 was a strange, exciting, and turbulent one for Rivera in many ways. Early in the new year Rivera's former lover, Tina Modotti, was accused of murdering a Cuban Communist named Julio Antonio Mella on a dark Mexico City street. Modotti had become romantically involved with Mella after her relationship with Rivera had ended. Mella had been forced to flee Cuba, leaving a wife and child behind, after his opposition to the dictatorship of Cuban ruler Gerardo Machado (1877-1945) put his life in danger.

Mella was murdered on the night of January 10, shortly after he and Modotti had left a Communist meeting. An unknown assassin—many historians believe the killer was one of Machado's agents—ambushed them as they were walking home and shot Mella twice. He died at a nearby hospital a few hours later.

Mexican authorities claimed that Modotti had murdered him in a crime of passion. As the investigation continued, police and prosecutors repeatedly smeared her name in leaks to newspapers. Friends and colleagues, however, refused to believe that she was guilty. They proclaimed her innocence and charged that the government was targeting her because of her Communist political beliefs. Within a matter of weeks, Rivera became her most prominent defender in the press. More importantly, he launched his own investigation of Mella's murder. Rivera's findings proved pivotal in finally securing Modotti's release. "My evidence . . . ripped apart the net of speculations in which the prosecution had hoped to entrap Tina,"[58] he later claimed.

Meeting Frida Kahlo

Around the same time that Rivera helped win Modotti's freedom, he entered into a serious romantic relationship with Frida Kahlo (1907-1954), a painter who was twenty-one years younger than him. Most biographers believe that the two artists met at a 1928 party hosted by Modotti (stories persist, however, that several years earlier, a group of students that included Kahlo played pranks on Rivera when he was painting a mural at the National Preparatory School). Rivera was immediately drawn to her unconventional beauty, intelligence, and self-confidence, while she was intrigued by his talent and charisma.

Soon after they met, Kahlo asked Rivera to look at some of her paintings and provide honest feedback. Rivera agreed, and after reviewing several canvases he assured her that she had the tools to be a fine artist. "The canvases revealed an unusual energy of expression, precise delineation of character, and true severity," Rivera recalled. "They had . . . an artistic personality of their own. They communicated a vital sensuality, complemented by a merciless yet sensitive power of observation. It was obvious to me that this girl was an authentic artist."[59]

Kahlo's past also fascinated Rivera. At the age of six she had been struck by polio, and this dreaded disease left her with a withered

Rivera assured Frida Kahlo that she had the skills to one day be a fine artist.

leg. As a youth, she had shown herself to be both bright and rebellious, and she expressed vague hopes for a career in medicine. On September 17, 1925, however, her life was changed forever by a horrifying accident. She was a passenger on a wooden bus that collided with an electric trolley car. The trolley was traveling at such a high speed that it tore the bus apart. The impact impaled Kahlo on a broken handrail, and by the time the wreckage of the bus came to a rest she had suffered horrible injuries to her spinal column, pelvis, collarbone, ribs, right leg, and reproductive organs.

Kahlo spent the next year in a full body cast strapped to a board. Unable to move anything but her hands, she devoted most of the next several months to painting. Her parents rigged a mirror so that she could view herself in bed, and she became accustomed to painting self-portraits. Kahlo returned to self-portraits again and again in later years, and these are the works for which she is best known today.

Another Marriage for Rivera

Dazzled by Kahlo's spirit and energy, Rivera cast aside his usual casual approach to romantic relationships. He frequently called on her at her parents' home, the so-called "Blue House," located in Coyoacán, a suburb of Mexico City. They also spent long nights making the rounds of downtown cafés, where they debated about politics, art, and love with their friends.

By the spring of 1929, Kahlo admitted to friends that she was in love with Rivera, who she called her "frog prince" because of his homely appearance. When he proposed marriage, she accepted immediately. They were married on August 29, 1929, in Mexico City. Rejecting the idea of a Catholic service because of Rivera's strong atheistic beliefs, they were united in a civil ceremony.

Rivera and Kahlo moved into a large and elegant house in one of Mexico City's finer neighborhoods. A constant parade of friends and colleagues showed up at their doorstep after they settled in. Some dropped by for an afternoon of wine and conversation. Others stayed for months at a time.

Pulled in Different Directions

Rivera and Kahlo were married at a time when political turmoil was once again wracking Mexico. On July 17, 1928, a religious fanatic had killed Mexican President Álvaro Obregón because of his anti-Catholic opinions. Plutarco Calles (1877-1945), who had been president before Obregón, quickly grabbed the reins of power once again. He installed a series of "puppets"—easily controlled politicians—in the president's office over the next several years and thus became the shadowy ruler of Mexico. During this time he forged a political party—the Partido Nacional Revolucionario (PNR)—which dominated Mexican politics under different names for the rest of the century.

Calles viewed communism as a potential threat to his power, so he regarded Rivera and other Mexican Communists with suspicion.

Rivera's reputation gave him greater freedom than most activists, however. In the spring of 1929, for example, he became director of his former school, the National School of Fine Arts at San Carlos Academy. Rivera immediately tossed out the old curriculum, which emphasized theory. Instead, he told the faculty to emphasize hands-on artmaking and to convey the importance of art that addressed the concerns of working-class people. Rivera even launched a special program to admit foundry workers, glassblowers, engravers, and other wage workers into the academy. He hoped that some of these changes would satisfy his fellow Communist activists, most of whom were suspicious of anyone who accepted any job associated with the government. Rivera's proposed changes alarmed government officials, however, and he was removed from the director's post in early 1930.

Despite criticism of his directorship, Rivera managed to stay in the government's good graces by accepting commissions to paint murals in official buildings. Most notably, Rivera accepted a commission to paint a mural depicting the history of Mexico on the staircase of the Presidential Palace, which is where Calles and other top governmental officials worked. This decision further angered Rivera's Communist colleagues. They saw Rivera's acceptance of a commission from Calles's government as an endorsement of its policies and actions, which included imprisonment of Communist activists.

When Rivera shrugged off his colleagues' demands that he show greater loyalty to the Communist cause, party officials responded by expelling him from the party in September 1929. Kahlo also resigned from the party in a show of support for her husband, but many long-time friends abandoned Rivera afterwards. Even Modotti, who owed her freedom to Rivera, condemned him for working with the enemy. "For a communist, there is only one way to relate to the party—maintain the party's line against everything and everybody, never for a moment doubting its correctness," Rivera explained years later.

> To hold a personal opinion at variance with the party's line means doubling one's burden. It means that, while continuing to fight the enemies of the revolution, one incurs the enmity of friends to whom the slightest difference of view appears as a betrayal.[60]

Working at the Palace of Cortez

Rivera's clashes with his former friends and colleagues took a heavy emotional toll on the artist. He even suffered a nervous breakdown, and Kahlo spent weeks nursing him back to health. Once he had regained his strength, he began his work on the controversial stairway project at the National Palace.

Rivera had barely begun his work on the frescoes at the National Palace when he received an intriguing job offer from Dwight Morrow, the U.S. ambassador to Mexico. Morrow was eager to make a symbolic gesture that would show Mexico that the United States was interested in improving relations between the two countries. To that end, he offered Rivera a generous commission ($12,000) to paint a mural at the Palace of Cortés in Cuernavaca in the Mexican state of Morelos. Rivera accepted, and in January 1930 he began painting at the Palace of Cortés, a fortress built by the infamous Spanish explorer, Hernán Cortés, who had conquered Mexico back in the sixteenth century. He spent the next several months dividing his time between the two projects.

The National Palace in Mexico City, Mexico, where Rivera worked on his controversial stairway project.

The Aztec World, a section of Rivera's mural that still can be found in the National Palace.

At Cuernavaca, Rivera's goal was to use frescoes to tell the history of the state of Morelos. As one scholar noted:

> the subject embraced many of his favorite themes—the idyllic life of the pre-Hispanic Indians, the villainous Spaniards, the cruelty and suffering imposed on the Indians, hard labor in the [sugar] cane fields, the heroic Zapata—and lots of tropical foliage.[61]

Rivera finished his frescoes at the Palace of Cortés in November 1930. Years later, he expressed satisfaction with his work there. "I chose to do scenes from the history of the region in sixteen consecutive panels, beginning with the Spanish conquest," he recalled in his autobiography.

> The episodes included the seizure of Cuernavaca by the Spaniards, the building of the palace by the conqueror, and the establishment of the sugar refineries. The concluding episode was the peasant revolt led by [Mexican revolutionary Emiliano] Zapata. . . . I took

care to authenticate every detail by exact research because I wanted to leave no opening for anyone to try to discredit the murals as a whole by the charge that any detail was a fabrication.[62]

To America

In late 1930, Rivera accepted two major commissions from American patrons. His willingness to accept "Yankee dollars" prompted the Communist press to attack him as an "agent of American imperialism"[63] and betrayer of communism. These accusations pained Rivera, but the opportunity to advance his career—and make his first visit to the fabled United States—was too attractive for him to pass up.

Rivera and Kahlo traveled to California in November 1930. The couple caused a stir as soon as they arrived in San Francisco. Rivera's famous face and massive bulk, combined with Kahlo's colorful peasant clothing and traditional necklaces and hairpieces, attracted press photographers and ordinary onlookers alike. The couple enjoyed the attention, but after a brief sightseeing tour Rivera turned his focus to the jobs that awaited him.

Rivera's commissions in California were from the American Stock Exchange Luncheon Club and the California School of Fine Arts. The title of the Stock Exchange fresco, which he completed in March 1931, was *Allegory of California*. This mural used a rich pageant of iconic images to show how the state's history and development was bound to its wealth of natural resources.

Rivera finished his fresco at the California School of Fine Arts in early June 1931. In terms of subject matter, this mural displayed the artist's usual interest in laborers and industrialization. In terms of design, however, it was one of his most innovative works. Its most dominant design element, wrote one biographer, was a portrait of:

> Rivera himself, seated on a painted scaffold with his back to the viewer, palette in one hand, brush in another, while four assistants labor on other aspects of the mural. The painted wall is about constructing the modern city, but it is also about constructing the modern mural.[64]

A Celebrity in New York

After finishing his fresco at the California School of Fine Arts, Rivera returned to Mexico City for three months. He spent most of his time working on his National Palace frescoes, but he also met with architect Juan O'Gorman. By the time their meeting was over, O'Gorman had agreed to design a combination studio/home for Rivera and Kahlo in the San Ángel section of Mexico City.

In October 1931, Rivera and Kahlo left Mexico for the United States once again. This time their destination was New York City, where the Museum of Modern Art was preparing a special exhibition of Rivera's artwork. As he roamed the streets of New York and attended dinner parties in his honor, Rivera remarked time and again on the skyscrapers, factories, bridges, and other engineering

The Museum of Modern Art in New York City, held a special exhibition of Rivera's art in 1931. More than 57,000 people attended the exhibition and it became one of the most popular art shows of the year.

and architectural marvels that formed the heart of America's cities. "Your engineers are your great artists and these highways are the most beautiful things I have seen in your beautiful country,"[65] he declared.

Rivera's one-man show was one of the hottest tickets of the year. More than 57,000 people attended the exhibition, which featured more than 150 of Rivera's paintings and drawings. In addition, Rivera's collected work was warmly reviewed by critics. By the time the show closed, "Rivera's place as one of the world's major painters was secure."[66]

Capturing the Spirit of American Industry

Rivera and Kahlo next set their sights on Detroit, Michigan, home of the American automobile industry. During his stay in San Francisco several months earlier, Rivera had discussed a possible mural project with William R. Valentiner, director of the Detroit Institute of Arts (DIA). By early 1932, when he arrived in Detroit, the Detroit Art Commission had extended a formal invitation to the muralist to create frescoes for the garden court of the DIA. Rivera happily accepted the commission, which would give him yet another opportunity to explore one of his favorite artistic themes: the impact of industrialization on human progress.

Rivera arrived in Detroit at the height of the Great Depression, an era of widespread unemployment and economic hardship in the United States and around the world. Yet the automobile factories and steel foundries of Detroit were still roaring, and Rivera's tours of these and other industrial facilities inspired him. During these weeks, he became friends with Edsel Ford, son of Ford Motor Company founder Henry Ford, and an important financial supporter of the DIA.

Rivera spent most of 1932 working on the DIA project. As the work progressed, Rivera's primary goal was to show in his murals how the industrial revolution could lift humankind to a better future. He also wanted his murals to convey his deep belief that the industrial marvels of the modern world were wonderful symbols of human creativity and ingenuity.

Communist Artist

"Señor Rivera has perpetuated a heartless hoax on his capitalist employer, Edsel Ford. Rivera was engaged to interpret Detroit; he has foisted on Mr. Ford and the Museum a Communist manifesto."

–Dr. George H. Derry, President of Marygrove College

Quoted in Donald Lochbiler, "Battle of the Garden Court." *DetroitNews.com*. Available at http://info.detnews.com/history.

To accomplish these goals, machines and other signs of the industrial age dominated large sections of Rivera's murals. "Diego had long believed [that painting] must absorb the machine if it was to find the style for this age," explained one scholar. "[It must learn to] master this marvelous new material and make it live again on walls as vividly and movingly as ever art had historical scenes, old legends, and religious parables."[67]

Rivera's Vision Defended

Rivera's *Detroit Industry* murals were unveiled to the public in March 1933. Most of the popular and critical response to the frescoes was positive.

> Engineers inspecting them expressed amazement at the sophisticated selection of key elements and the fidelity of reproduction. Nonmechanical viewers were surprised at the way in which Rivera could make turbines, conveyor belts and stamping machines look sensual.[68]

The murals did not entirely escape criticism, however. Some viewers felt that Rivera's work carried a dark suggestion that technological progress threatened human individuality. In addition, several religious leaders in the Detroit area strongly objected to one panel that seemed to picture a Christ child being vaccinated by a scientist in a setting that was part-laboratory, part-manger. These critics denounced Rivera as both an atheist and a Communist— which of course he was—and demanded that the offensive fresco be removed.

The museum directors and Edsel Ford responded to the criticism by issuing strong statements of support for Rivera. These statements did not noticeably relieve tensions. When some Detroit union leaders indicated that they were willing to use members to guard the mural, however, the public outcry against the DIA murals faded away. Today, the *Detroit Industry* frescoes rank among Rivera's most famous and critically acclaimed murals.

Detroit Industry Murals

"Rivera's reverence for technology meant that he was a particularly good choice of artist for Detroit's automotive elite, but a closer examination of the *Detroit Industry* murals reveals that he was aware of the darker side of technological progress."

Saronne Rubyan-Ling, "The Detroit Murals of Diego Rivera." *History Today*, April 1996.

Rivera and Rockefeller

Rivera and Kahlo left Detroit in late March for yet another waiting mural commission. They returned to New York City, where the famous businessman Nelson Rockefeller had secured Rivera's services to paint a mural for the new RCA Building in Rockefeller Center.

The couple arrived in New York with heavy hearts, however. Rivera's grueling work schedule back in Detroit had brought waves of poor health and shocking weight loss. In addition, Kahlo had suffered a miscarriage during their stay in Detroit. This was an emotionally devastating loss to Rivera's young wife, who had always hoped that she would be able to bear children despite the injuries she had suffered earlier in life.

Prior to his arrival in New York, Rivera had agreed to create a mural that would be titled *Man at the Crossroads Looking with Hope and High Vision to the Choosing of a New and Better Future*. Rockefeller believed that the mural Rivera would paint would be inspiring, but for some reason he failed to anticipate that it might also reflect some of the painter's Communist beliefs. As Rivera's

A Life in the Limelight

Nelson A. Rockefeller was born into one of America's richest families on July 8, 1908, in Bar Harbor, Maine. His grandfather, John D. Rockefeller Sr., had famously built a fortune as founder of the Standard Oil Company, and his father, John Jr., had been an effective manager of the family's financial empire.

As a young man, Nelson worked as an executive for several family businesses. By the late 1930s he was also well known throughout New York as a generous supporter of the arts. In the 1940s and 1950s Rockefeller worked for the U.S. government and developed a keen understanding of foreign affairs and other public policy issues.

In 1958, Rockefeller won the first of four consecutive terms as Republican governor of the state of New York. During these years he became well known for his strong support for education, transportation and housing, environmental protection, and the arts. Three different attempts to win the Republican nomination for the presidency failed, however. The closest he came to the Oval Office—a life-long dream for him—was the vice presidency; he served as Gerald Ford's vice president from August 1974 to January 1977. Rockefeller died of a heart attack in New York City on January 26, 1979.

Nelson A. Rockefeller was a strong supporter of the arts among other things.

A section of Rivera's Man at the Crossroads Looking with Hope and High Vision *that reflected some of the painter's beliefs. Originally commissioned by Nelson Rockefeller, the mural was later destroyed because of its controversial nature.*

work progressed, however, he defiantly included several figures and scenes that almost seemed designed to taunt Rockefeller, who was one of the country's wealthiest and best-known capitalists. These images ranged from peasants and workers marching under a Communist flag to a portrait of Vladimir Lenin, the first premier of the Soviet Union.

As rumors about Rivera's mural began to swirl around New York, Rockefeller decided that he needed to intervene. Noting that Lenin's face had not appeared anywhere in the sketch of the mural that Rivera had submitted for approval, Rockefeller approached the painter and asked him with as much diplomacy as he could muster to remove the famous Communist revolutionary's face from the mural. Rivera flatly refused the request. The only compromise he offered was to add a portrait of Abraham Lincoln or some other American leader to the fresco.

Angry and embarrassed, Rockefeller ordered Rivera and his assistants out of the building. The unfinished mural was covered in heavy canvas sheets for six months, then destroyed. One year later, Rivera expressed outrage over this series of events.

> Tens of millions of people were informed that the nation's richest man had ordered the veiling of the portrait of an individual named Vladimir Ilyitch Lenin . . . because a painter had represented him in a fresco as a Leader, guiding the exploited masses towards a new social order based on the suppression of classes, organization, love and peace among human beings.[69]

Portrait of America

After being kicked out of the RCA Building, Rivera used the commission money he had already received from Rockefeller to create a fresco at the New Workers' School in New York City. This school was directed by Bertram Wolfe, a future Rivera biographer. Rivera selected the school for his mural because it had emerged as a center of anti-Stalinist Communist activity in the eastern United States. Like many other dedicated Communists, Rivera had become convinced by the mid-1930s that Soviet Premier Joseph Stalin had abandoned core Communist ideals. Rivera and his fellow "anti-Stalinists" believed that once the murderous Stalin was removed from power in the Soviet Union, the true age of communism could begin.

Rivera painted a total of twenty-one frescoes at the New Workers' School. The collective name the painter gave to the murals was *Portrait of America*. Most of the panels depicted famous events in American history, but Rivera put a heavy emphasis on acts of oppression (such as exploitation of Native Americans and African Americans) and mistreatment of working-class people. Rivera also made a point of including a portrait of Lenin in a prominent position in the mural.

Muralism Reaches New Heights of Popularity

Rivera returned to Mexico in December 1933. By the time he left the United States, mural painting had surged in popularity across

Thomas Hart Benton, American Muralist

The most obvious twentieth-century American counterpart to Diego Rivera was Thomas Hart Benton, a muralist who created huge portraits of American life for much of his career. Born on April 15, 1889, in Neosho, Missouri, Benton studied at the Chicago Art Institute. He spent his early career struggling to make ends meet in Paris and New York before finally finding success as a muralist.

Benton moved back to the Midwest, where he took a job as an instructor at the Kansas City Art Institute. His most famous student was Jackson Pollock, but Pollock's later abstract expressionist paintings were quite unlike those that brought Benton public renown. Benton was a champion of Regionalism, a movement that celebrated American history and rural life. As the PBS series "American Stories" noted in an episode devoted to Benton, he specialized in "huge murals and audacious paintings that reflected raw American life, some of it historical, mostly of ordinary folk caught in the throes of hard work."

Benton died in his studio in Kansas City on January 19, 1975. Many of Benton's best-known murals are still in place today, including works at the Missouri State Capitol in Jefferson City and the Truman Library in Independence, Missouri.

the country. Established artists such as Ben Shahn (1898-1969), who worked as an assistant to Rivera in the United States, and Thomas Hart Benton (1889-1975) were joined by many other artists around the United States who received commissions to transform blank building walls into colorful frescoes.

The mural craze received vital support from President Franklin D. Roosevelt and his New Deal programs. One of the primary goals of these programs was to lift the burden of the Great Depression by getting unemployed Americans working on federally funded projects. The first of these programs in the realm of cultural support was the Public Works of Art Project. This program, which was launched in December 1933, included commissions for young artists to create murals on public spaces around the country.

Some of these artists had worked with Rivera in Mexico or the United States. Others had been influenced by Rivera or fellow Mexican muralists José Clemente Orozco and David Alfaro Siqueiros, both of whom were also working in the United States during this period. Rivera was easily the most famous of the "Big Three," however. "By 1934, Rivera had, virtually single-handedly, forged a strong mural tradition," wrote one scholar. "He was the best, and certainly the most famous, muralist in the Americas, and his walls had become the standard against which those who aspired to be muralists were judged (or judged themselves). Rivera was the role model both stylistically and ideologically."[70]

Benton later acknowledged that Rivera, Siqueiros, and Orozco helped him gain greater acceptance for his own frescoes. More importantly, Rivera and his countrymen influenced his own attitudes toward muralism. "I saw in the Mexican effort a profound and much-needed redirection of art towards its ancient humanistic functions," Benton said. "The Mexican concern with publicly significant meanings and with the pageant of Mexican national life corresponded perfectly with what I had in mind for art in the United States."[71]

Chapter 5

Rivera and Kahlo

During the last two decades of Diego Rivera's life, his relationship with fellow painter Frida Kahlo received as much public attention as his art work. This change was due in part to the fact that Rivera created most of his greatest masterpieces in the 1920s and early 1930s. It was also due, however, to the fascinating and turbulent union of the two artists. They angered and humiliated one another on numerous occasions during their years together. Yet in the end they always returned to one another because each of them saw the other as a soulmate.

Rivera's Murals at the National Palace

Rivera and Kahlo returned to Mexico from the United States in late 1933. Upon his return, Rivera turned his attention to his gigantic mural at the National Palace, a work that he had begun four years earlier. He completed the stairway mural in November 1935, but added other murals in various corners of the palace for the next twenty years. The entire work was titled *Mexico: Yesterday, Today, and Tomorrow.*

By the time it was complete, Rivera's staircase mural had become one of the crowning achievements of his career. As one scholar

Part of Rivera's mural titled Mexico: Yesterday Today and Tomorrow, *which critics claim to be one of the crowning achievements of Rivera's career.*

noted, the mural provides a visually stunning summary of Mexico's history and future potential:

> Rivera envisioned the sweep of time as an immense and colorful panorama, starting with the Pre-Hispanic period on the right, and moving leftward, through the conquest, the War of Independence, the revolution and finally, on the left, to the present and even the future. . . . With his gargantuan appetite for life and his irrepressible curiosity, he wanted to include everything. As a result, his mural teems with so much detail that the viewer is at first overwhelmed. One must read his mural like a book, examining first one part and then another, until one forms a vivid picture of the story of Mexico.[72]

After completing the staircase mural, Rivera spent the rest of the 1930s concentrating on his easel work. These works did not attract as much attention as his murals of the early 1930s, but many of them were of exceptional quality. It was also during this time, wrote one biographer, that Rivera:

> became the painter of the Indian, the artist who burned into the world's consciousness the image of the indigenous people of Mexico. . . . Rivera made the subject his own. In many oil paintings, hundreds of watercolors, and perhaps thousands of pencil and ink drawings he evoked the dignity, honor, and beauty of the Indians.[73]

A Stormy Marriage

This productive period in Rivera's painting career came at the same time that his personal life had become more chaotic than ever before. In the years that had passed since their 1929 marriage, River and Kahlo's relationship had become a very complicated one. Angered by his inability or unwillingness to remain faithful to her, Kahlo had also begun looking outside of marriage for companionship.

Yet despite periods of intense anger at her husband, Kahlo never stopped loving Rivera. As one of her biographers wrote:

> The pivot of her existence was her desire to be a good wife for him. This did not mean eclipsing herself: Rivera admired strong and independent women; he expected Frida to have her own ideas, her own friends, her own activities. He encouraged her painting and the development of her unique style. . . . That she tried to earn her living so as not to depend on him for support and that she kept her maiden name pleased him. And if he did not open car doors for her, he opened worlds: he was the great maestro; she chose to be his admiring compañera (female companion).[74]

Even so, Rivera's selfish ways sometimes cut Kahlo so deeply that she had to flee from his sight. In 1934, for example, Kahlo discovered that Rivera was having an affair with her younger sister Cristina, to whom she had always been especially close. This discovery, which came around the same time that doctors warned Kahlo that sexual intercourse could actually be dangerous to her health, prompted her to flee to New York for several weeks. Years later, Rivera expressed deep self-loathing for his treatment of Kahlo. "If I loved a woman, the more I loved her, the more I wanted to hurt her,"[75] he wrote. "Frida was only the most obvious victim of this disgusting trait."

Lázaro Cárdenas

Mexican revolutionary leader and president Lázaro Cárdenas was born on May 21, 1895, in the city of Jiquilpan in the Mexican state of Michoacán. Raised in a working-class family, he received little formal schooling after his father died when he was in his mid-teens. Yet the years of schooling he did receive made a lasting impact on him, for he was a great champion of education during his presidency.

Cárdenas fought in the Mexican Revolution, and in 1920 he supported Alvaro Obregón's successful campaign to take control of the country. In 1923 Cárdenas was named a brigadier general in the Mexican Army. In 1928 he was appointed governor of Michoacán. Six years later he was hand-picked by Mexican politician Plutarco Calles to assume the presidency.

Calles assumed that he could control Cárdenas, but he was badly mistaken. Instead Cárdenas launched a series of ambitious political reforms during his six-year term of office, including the distribution of millions of acres of land to Mexico's poorest citizens. He also exiled Calles to the United States. Today, Cárdenas is regarded by scholars and ordinary Mexicans alike as one of the most principled and dedicated public servants in Mexican history.

Lázaro Cárdenas was a great supporter of education during his presidency.

A New Age in Mexico

The early years of Rivera and Kahlo's turbulent marriage unfolded at the same time that a new political age was dawning in Mexico. In December 1934 Lázaro Cárdenas (1895-1970) assumed the presidency of Mexico. Like most other Mexicans, Rivera assumed that Cárdenas would follow the wishes of his patron Plutarco Calles, who had ruled the country for the last several years through a succession of presidential "puppets." Within a few months of his inauguration, however, it became clear that Cárdenas was both tough and idealistic. He initiated major land reforms to help Mexico's poor and began laying the groundwork to put the country's oil industry under government control. Alarmed by the president's surprising independent streak, Calles began plotting to remove him. Cárdenas struck first, however, by sending Calles and his top aides into exile.

Cárdenas remained true to his ethical principles and radical political ideas throughout his six-year term, which ended in 1940. "He was always on the side of the poor and the oppressed, functioning practically and without publicity on their behalf," confirmed one historian. "He never revenged himself upon his enemies. He did not enrich himself. He acted upon principle."[76]

Cárdenas also lifted legal restrictions against the Mexican Communist Party, which had been outlawed by Calles in 1929. Instead of showing gratitude, however, party leaders attacked the president. Their hostility toward Cárdenas stemmed from a belief that the president's progressive policies were sapping popular support for their own cause. In addition, many Mexican Communists gave their allegiance to Soviet strongman Joseph Stalin, not their own countrymen. As a result, they expressed outright rage when Cárdenas gave Leon Trotsky, Stalin's arch-enemy, permission to enter the country.

Rivera and Trotsky

Rivera was an enthusiastic supporter of Trotsky, who had been in danger from Stalin's agents since the late 1920s, when he was expelled from the Soviet Union. In the mid-1930s, for example, Rivera joined the International Communist League, which was closely aligned to Trotsky. When the Soviets pressured

Norway to expel Trotsky from their country in 1936, Rivera asked Cárdenas to grant asylum to the Russian revolutionary in Mexico. The president approved the request, and in January 1937 Trotsky and his wife Natalia arrived in Veracruz.

Rivera arranged for Trotsky and his wife to live in the Kahlo family's famous Blue House in Coyoacán, in the suburbs of Mexico City. He also supervised the transformation of the Blue House into a fortress of sorts to better protect Trotsky from assassins. Over the next two years, the painter and the revolutionary spent long hours socializing and debating over politics. They and their wives even went on a long vacation together. In the spring of 1939, however, relations between the two men took a dramatic turn for the worse.

Rivera and Trotsky parted ways for two reasons. First, the two men came to recognize that they had major differences in terms of their political philosophies. Second—and most importantly—Rivera became convinced that his wife and Trotsky were having an affair.

Although some scholars are uncertain whether Kahlo and Trotsky actually conducted an affair, Rivera had no doubts. He

Left to Right: Andre Breton, Diego Rivera, Leon Trotsky, and Jacqueline Lamba Snark. Between 1937 and 1939 Rivera and Trotsky spent long hours socializing and debating politics.

Leon Trotsky

Leon Trotsky was born Lev Davidovich Bronstein on November 7, 1879, in Yanovka, Urkaine, which was then part of Russia. As a teenager he became a member of the Social Democratic Party, an early version of the Russian Communist Party. This underground movement opposed the czars that ruled Russia at that time and called for a socialist form of government. During his twenties he was exiled to Siberia for his anti-government actions, but he escaped and became a leading member of the Bolsheviks, a faction of the Social Democratic Party.

During the early years of the twentieth century, Russia was wracked with political turmoil. This unrest ultimately resulted in the Russian Revolution of 1917, in which the Bolsheviks—led by Vladimir Lenin and Trotsky—seized power over the country and instituted a Communist form of government. Trotsky spent the next several years as a diplomat and general. After Lenin died in 1924, Joseph Stalin moved decisively to take the reins of power. Trotsky was forced into exile in 1928. He spent the next several years attacking Stalin from abroad. On August 21, 1940, Trotsky died in Mexico City from an attack from a Stalinist agent.

angrily kicked Trotsky out of the Blue House. A few months later Rivera and Kahlo filed for divorce and she traveled to New York and Paris to support her own fast-rising art career. On return visits to Mexico City, Kahlo and Rivera appeared together in public on several occasions. She tried to appear happy and content at these times, but in reality she had become heavily dependent on alcohol to dull the terrible pain she lived with on a daily basis.

Trotsky, meanwhile, remained in Mexico. He and Rivera traded insults in the papers until May 24, 1940, when the pro-Stalinist Mexican painter David Alfaro Siqueiros launched a scheme to murder Trotsky. The assassination attempt failed, but news of the plot convinced Rivera that his own life might be in danger from pro-Stalinist agents—or from Trotsky supporters who believed that he had been one of the plotters. He decided to return to the United States until conditions in Mexico calmed down. By this time Rivera had begun secretly passing information about Mexican Communist leaders to the U.S. State Department. His connections with the

State Department enabled him to quickly obtain a travel visa, and by June 1940 he had safely arrived in San Francisco. Two months later, he learned that Trotsky had been murdered in Mexico by a Stalinist with an ice pick.

Back in the United States

Rivera spent the next six months in San Francisco. He spent much of this time working on a mural for the Golden Gate International Exposition. Each day, curious fairgoers watched Rivera and his attendants as they toiled on the mural, which was titled *Marriage of the Artistic Expression of the North and South on This Continent*. When the exposition ended, the mural was packed up. It remained in storage for several years before being put on permanent display at the Art Auditorium of San Francisco City College.

Kahlo joined Rivera in San Francisco in September 1940. Emotionally battered by Trotsky's death—and several hours of intense questioning she had endured at the hands of Mexican investigators—Kahlo spent her first couple of weeks in a hospital. She then traveled with a friend to New York, where she stayed for most of the fall. Rivera spoke with her often by telephone, though, and by the end of the year he was peppering her with proposals that they re-marry. Kahlo finally accepted on the conditions that they keep their finances separate and have no sexual relations with one another. Rivera accepted the deal, and on December 8, 1940—Rivera's fifty-fourth birthday—they remarried in San Francisco.

In February 1941, Rivera and Kahlo returned to Mexico. They lived together in the Blue House, but Rivera still spent many of his hours at his studio in San Ángel. For the next few years, this arrangement seemed to suit them both.

Kahlo's Accidents

"I have suffered two serious accidents in my life. "One in which a streetcar ran over me. . . . The other accident is Diego."

Frida Kahlo, quoted in Martha Zamora, *Frida Kahlo: The Brush of Anguish.* San Francisco: Chronicle Books, 1990, p. 50.

Making and Spending Money

Rivera returned to mural work in the early 1940s. Instead of creating frescoes in public places as he had done in the past, however, most of his mural efforts during this period were private commissions painted for the homes and businesses of

Rivera's painting which is titled Portrait of Dolores Olmedo. *During his later years, Rivera supported himself by painting portraits of wealthy individuals such as this.*

rich admirers. Many of his easel paintings from these years were portraits commissioned by wealthy individuals as well.

This shift was due in part to motion pictures, which had exploded in popularity over the previous decade. Rivera and other painters recognized that motion pictures could reach far more people than public murals ever could, and they sensed that interest in murals was slipping. More importantly, Rivera seized on these commissions because he was spending money on pre-Columbian art and other things as fast as he made it. "Rivera needed money. He turned to the same market that had supported other great painters for centuries: the rich. He painted rich men. He painted the wives of rich men."[77] In return, the wealthy landowners and industrialists that hired him could boast that the most famous painter in Mexico had painted their portrait.

In 1941, Rivera's collection of pre-Columbian art became so large that he decided to build an Aztec-style pyramid to house all the artifacts. Even before it was completed, this building became yet another of Rivera's studios. Meanwhile, in 1943, Rivera accepted a government offer to teach composition and painting at the Colegio Nacional's prestigious School of Painting and Sculpture. Other well-known artists who joined the faculty around this time included Kahlo and Orozco.

Dream of a Sunday Afternoon

In 1947, Rivera painted his last great mural. This private commission, for Mexico City's famous Hotel del Prado, showed that when he was inspired, Rivera could still create enduring art.

The title of the Hotel del Prado mural was *Dream of a Sunday Afternoon in Alameda Park*. For this work, Rivera returned to one of his favorite subjects: the history of his homeland. But he also scattered intensely personal touches into the fresco, such as portraits of Kahlo, legendary Mexican engraver José Guadalupe Posada—and Rivera himself as a young boy. "*Dream* . . . is one of Rivera's greatest masterpieces, suffused with affection, sunlight, nostalgia," wrote one scholar. "He paints even the villains of Mexican history with a certain radiance, as if acknowledging that without villains, history has no drama."[78]

For Dream of a Sunday Afternoon in Alameda Park *Rivera returned to his favorite subject, the history of his homeland. This piece would be his last great mural of his career.*

Dream of a Sunday Afternoon in Alameda Park also brought Rivera a wave of criticism from Catholic leaders and believers. One of the many characters featured in the mural carried a scroll that proclaimed *Dios No Existe* ("God Does Not Exist"). The controversy delighted Rivera, but it horrified the hotel owners. The ownership promptly hid the mural behind a series of hastily erected drapes. The mural remained hidden for the next nine years, until Rivera painted over the offensive phrase.

The Death of Frida Kahlo

By the late 1940s, Kahlo's physical condition had declined so badly that she was confined to bed for months at a time. In 1950, she spent virtually the entire year in the hospital. One of the only events that lifted her spirits during these years was her readmittance into the Communist Party in 1948. Rivera begged again and again to be accepted back into the party as well, but his former colleagues turned him down each time. Some historians even speculate that party leaders might have readmitted Kahlo to make Rivera feel even worse about his outsider status.

In 1952, Rivera painted his last major mural, *The Nightmare of War and the Dream of Peace.* The mural amounted to little more than a desperate attempt to bribe his way back into the Communist Party's favor, for it featured portraits of both Joseph Stalin and Chinese Communist leader Mao Zedong (1893-1976) in heroic poses. The mural was so controversial and poorly done, that the sponsor, the Instituto Nacional de Bellas Artes, refused to show it.

In August 1953, Kahlo's right leg was amputated. She spent her last few months in a haze of drugs and alcohol as she tried to dull the horrible pain that wracked her body. In early July she contracted pneumonia, and she died on July 13. The official cause of death on her death certificate was a "pulmonary embolism"—a blood clot in one of her lungs—but most scholars believe that she died of a drug overdose. Some friends, family members, and colleagues believed that Kahlo's death was a suicide, but others insisted that she never would have taken that path to end her pain.

Rivera used Kahlo's memorial service to show his loyalty to the Communist Party. Soon after the service he was readmitted to the party.

As word of Kahlo's death spread through town, friends, relatives, and admirers crowded into the house. Rivera refused to meet with them. Instead, he locked himself in their bedroom to mourn in private. Rivera later described the day of Kahlo's death as the worst one of his life. "Too late, I realized the most wonderful part of my life had been my love for Frida,"[79] he said.

Fascination with Frida Kahlo

Throughout her marriage to Diego Rivera, painter Frida Kahlo was accustomed to her husband receiving the lion's share of attention from critics, fellow artists, and members of their social circle. Her paintings, most of which were unflattering self-portraits, received some critical praise, and she even had a few successful solo exhibitions of her work. Until her death in 1954, however, Kahlo always worked in Rivera's shadow.

In the 1980s and 1990s, however, this situation became reversed. Rivera's contributions to twentieth-century art were still recognized, but Kahlo and her body of work became the subject of intense interest. The value of some of Kahlo's best-known paintings rose meteorically, and a flurry of biographies and documentaries about her art and her difficult life were released. In 2002, Hollywood even produced a hit movie about her life starring Mexican beauty Salma Hayak as Kahlo. Today, she is one of the most revered and popular female artists of the twentieth century.

Although she lived in the shadow of Diego Rivera during her lifetime, after her death, Frida Kahlo came into her own and people began to appreciate her own body of work.

A special memorial service for Kahlo was scheduled for the Palace of Fine Arts, the premier art museum in Mexico. Rivera used the service—and Kahlo's coffin—as a prop to show his loyalty to the Communist cause. He arranged to have a red flag with a golden hammer and sickle, the symbols of international communism, draped over her casket. A few weeks later, Rivera was finally readmitted into the Mexican Communist Party.

Rivera's Last Months

In July 1955, Rivera married Emma Hurtado, who had been his main art dealer for the previous decade. Around this same time he was diagnosed with cancer. In August, Rivera and his new bride left for Moscow after receiving an invitation to visit the city from the Moscow Fine Arts Academy. Rivera and Hurtado were gone for several months as they visited many of the largest cities in Communist Eastern Europe and the Soviet Union. Health problems continued to plague Rivera, however, and he was forced to spend part of his vacation in a hospital.

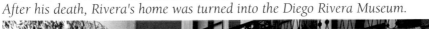

After his death, Rivera's home was turned into the Diego Rivera Museum.

Rivera and Hurtado returned to Mexico in April 1956. A short time after his return, Rivera renounced his famous atheism and declared that he had decided to return to the Roman Catholic Church. "I admire the Virgin of Guadalupe," he explained. "She was the standard of Zapata, and she is the symbol of my country. It is my desire to gratify my countrymen, the Mexican Catholics, who comprise 96 percent of the population of the country."[80]

In July 1957, Rivera opened the Kahlo family's famed Blue House to the public as the Frida Kahlo Museum. Two months later, on November 24, 1957, he suffered a fatal heart attack at his studio. In accordance with his will, Rivera's collection of pre-Hispanic art was given to the people of Mexico. A special memorial service was held in his honor at the Palace of Fine Arts. His ashes were then placed by special presidential order in Mexico's famous Rotunda of Illustrious Men, a memorial area reserved for the nation's greatest heroes.

Lyrical Art

"In both painting and manner [Rivera] could display a great gentleness, and in much of his painting there was a lyrical quality."

William Weber Johnson, "The Tumultuous Life and Times of the Painter Diego Rivera." *Smithsonian*, February 1986, p 36.

Leaving His Mark

Historians and scholars admit that Rivera's reputation as a major artist has eroded somewhat since his death a half-century ago. Some critics have panned his murals as overrated political propaganda. The arrival of abstract expressionism and other artistic movements also led some people to dismiss his entire body of work as a "creaky artifact"[81] of a distant past. Rivera's place in art history was further complicated in the 1990s, when critical and popular attention to the art of his wife, Frida Kahlo, rose dramatically.

Despite everything, however, Rivera is still acknowledged to be the most famous painter in Mexican history—and the champion

Diego Rivera is still acknowledged as being one of the most famous artists in Mexican history. Many of his pieces can still be seen around the world.

of the Mexican Muralist Movement. Many of Rivera's most famous murals still can be seen by residents and visitors to Mexico City, and dozens of his easel paintings and sketches can be viewed at Mexico City's Museum of Plastic Arts and the Diego Rivera Museum in Guanajuato, Mexico. Others are scattered in museums and private residences around the world.

Rivera's masterpiece, Detroit Industry, also continues to grace the inner walls of the Detroit Institute of Arts in downtown Detroit. Through this work and the many powerful frescoes that remain on display in his native Mexico, "Rivera continues to communicate his ideas and concepts with dazzling force and beauty, through images, colors, and truly masterful composition," wrote Javier Barros Valero, the former director of Mexico's Instituto Nacional de Bellas Artes. "Through these murals, his aspirations, his beliefs, and his affections are seen in works that are, without a doubt, among the greatest monuments of the art of [the twentieth] century."[82]

Important Dates

1886
Diego Rivera and twin brother José are born on December 13 in Guanajuato, Mexico.

1899
Rivera begins taking classes at San Carlos Academy in Mexico City.

1907
Rivera arrives in Europe to study art.

1910
Rivera returns to Mexico, but leaves for Europe early the following year, just as the Mexican Revolution (1910-1920) begins to intensify.

1913
Rivera begins his first experimentation with the art form known as cubism.

1921
Rivera returns to Mexico and begins his career as a muralist.

1928
Rivera completes his famous mural work at the National Education building in Mexico City.

1929
Rivera marries Frida Kahlo; a few weeks later he is expelled from the Mexico Communist Party.

1933
Rivera completes *Detroit Industry,* his most famous mural in the United States.

1934
Rivera's controversial mural at New York's RCA Building is destroyed by order of Nelson Rockefeller.

1937
Russian revolutionary Leon Trotsky arrives in Mexico under the sponsorship of Rivera.

1940
Rivera and Kahlo divorce, then remarry in December; Trotsky is assassinated in Mexico City.

1947
Rivera begins work on *Dream of a Sunday Afternoon in Alameda Park*, his final masterpiece.

1954
Kahlo dies after years of poor health; Rivera marries Emma Hurtado one year later.

1957
Rivera dies of heart failure in Mexico City on November 24.

Notes

Introduction

1. Pete Hamill, "Viva Rivera!" *Los Angeles Magazine*, January 1997, p. 61.
2. Michael Kimmelman, "Sleeping with the Enemy." *New York Times*, December 20, 1998.
3. William Weber Johnson, "The Tumultuous Life and Times of the Painter Diego Rivera." *Smithsonian*, February 1986, p. 36.
4. Bertram D. Wolfe, *The Fabulous Life of Diego Rivera*. New York: Stein and Day, 1963.
5. *American Masters: Diego Rivera*. Available online at www.pbs.org/americanmasters/database/rivera_d.html.
6. Linda Downs. "Preface." In *Diego Rivera,* ed. Linda Downs and Detroit Institute of Arts. New York: W.W. Norton, 1986, p. 15.
7. Linda Downs, *Diego Rivera: The Detroit Industry Murals*. New York: Norton, 2000, p. 27.

Chapter 1: Born to be an Artist

8. Johnson, "The Tumultuous Life and Times of the Painter Diego Rivera," p. 36.
9. Diego Rivera, *My Art, My Life*. New York: Dover, 1991, p.3
10. Rivera, *My Art, My Life*, p. 3.
11. Cynthia Newman Helms, ed. *Diego Rivera: A Retrospective*. New York: W.W. Norton, 1986, p. 25.
12. Wolfe, *The Fabulous Life of Diego Rivera*.
13. Rivera, My Art, My Life, p. 9.
14. Quoted in Alfredo Cardona Peña, *Conversaciones con Diego Rivera*. Mexico City: Editorial Diana, 1980, p. 43.
15. Rivera, *My Art, My Life*, p. 11.
16. Patrick Marnham, *Dreaming With His Eyes Open: A Life of Diego Rivera*. New York: Knopf, 1998.
17. Pete Hamill, *Diego Rivera*. New York: Abrams, 1999, p. 18.

18. Jean Charlot, *Mexican Art and the Academy of San Carlos,* 1785-1915. Austin: University of Texas Press, 1962, p. 42.
19. Hamill, *Diego Rivera,* p. 25.
20. Rivera, *My Art, My Life,* pp. 17-18.
21. Rivera, *My Art, My Life.*
22. Patrick Frank, "Charlot, Posada, and Mexican Life." In Jose Guadalupe Posada: *My Mexico.* Exhibition catalogue. Honolulu: University of Hawaii Art Gallery, 2000.
23. Hamill, *Diego Rivera,* p. 17.

Chapter 2: Learning from the Masters

24. Quoted in Andrea Kettenmann, *Diego Rivera.* Cologne: Taschen, 1997, p. 13.
25. Hamill, *Diego Rivera,* p. 31.
26. Rivera, *My Art, My Life,* p. 27
27. Hamill, *Diego Rivera,* p. 38.
28. Jorge Hernández Campos, "The Influence of the Classical Tradition, Cézanne, and Cubism on Rivera's Artistic Development." In *Diego Rivera,* edited by Linda Downs and Detroit Institute of Arts. New York: W.W. Norton, 1986, p. 122.
29. Rivera, *My Art, My Life,* 58.
30. Hamill, *Diego Rivera,* p. 52.
31. James Cockcroft, *Diego Rivera.* New York: Chelsea House, p. 44.
32. Cockcroft, *Diego Rivera,* p. 46.
33. Rivera, *My Art, My Life,* p. 60.
34. Rivera, *My Art, My Life,* p. 60.
35. Rivera, *My Art, My Life,* p. 65
36. Angeline Beloff, *Memorias.* Mexico City: Universidad Nacional Autónoma de México, 1986.
37. Rivera, *My Art, My Life,* p. 68.
38. Rivera, *My Art, My Life,* p. 68.
39. Quoted in Florence Arquin, *Diego Rivera: The Shaping of an Artist.* Norman, OK: University of Oklahoma Press, 1971, p. 86.
40. Cockcroft. *Diego Rivera,* p. 60.
41. Campos, "The Influence of the Classical Tradition, Cézanne,

and Cubism on Rivera's Artistic Development," p.123.

42. Rivera, *My Art, My Life*, p. 58.

Chapter 3: Inspiring Change in Mexico

43. Luis Cardoza y Aragón,. "Diego Rivera's Murals in Mexico and the United States." In *Diego Rivera*, ed. Linda Downs and Detroit Institute of Arts. New York: W.W. Norton, 1986, p. 186.

44. Quoted in Helms, *Diego Rivera: A Retrospective*, p. 21.

45. Rivera, *My Art, My Life*, p. 73.

46. Hamill, *Diego Rivera*, p. 92.

47. Jean Charlot, *The Mexican Mural Renaissance, 1920-1925.* New Haven, CT: Yale University Press, 1962, p. 257.

48. Charlot. *The Mexican Mural Renaissance, 1920-1925,* p. 257.

49. Quoted in Ida Rodríguez-Pramplini, "Rivera's Concept of History." In *Diego Rivera.* ed. by Linda Downs and Detroit Institute of Arts. New York: W.W. Norton, 1986, p. 131-32.

50. Rivera. *My Art, My Life*, p. 83.

51. Hamill, *Diego Rivera*, p. 131.

52. Hamill, *Diego Rivera*, p. 98.

53. Wolfe, *The Fabulous Life of Diego Rivera*, p. 169.

54. Alejandro Anreus, "Diego Rivera," *Art Nexus*, May-July 1999.

55. Hamill, "Viva Rivera!" p. 61.

56. Quoted in Raquel Tibol, ed. *Arte y politica/Diego Rivera.* Mexico City: Editorial Grijalbo, 1979, p. 27.

57. Rivera, *My Art, My Life*, p. 83.

Chapter 4: Creating Controversy in America

58. Rivera, *My Art, My Life*, p. 97.

59. Rivera, *My Art, My Life*, pp. 102-03.

60. Rivera, *My Art, My Life*, p. 99.

61. Johnson, "The Tumultuous Life and Times of the Painter Diego Rivera," p. 36.

62. Rivera. *My Art, My Life*, p. 99.

63. Johnson. "The Tumultuous Life and Times of the Painter Diego Rivera," p. 36.

64. Hamill, *Diego Rivera*, p. 149.
65. Wolfe, *Diego. Rivera: His Life and Times*. New York: Knopf, 1939, p. 314.
66. Johnson. "The Tumultuous Life and Times of the Painter Diego Rivera," p. 36.
67. Wolfe, *The Fabulous Life of Diego Rivera*, p. 305-06.
68. Johnson. "The Tumultuous Life and Times of the Painter Diego Rivera," p. 36.
69. Quoted in Bertram D. Wolfe, *Portrait of America*. New York: Covici, Friede, 1934.
70. Francis V. O'Connor, "The Influence of Diego Rivera on the Art of the United States during the 1930s and After." In *Diego Rivera*, ed. Linda Downs and Detroit Institute of Arts. New York: W.W. Norton, 1986, p. 186.
71. Thomas Hart Benton, *An American in Art: A Professional and Technical Autobiography*. Lawrence: University Press of Kansas, 1969, p. 61.

Chapter 5: Rivera and Kahlo

72. Hayden Herrera, "José Clemente Orozco and Diego Rivera: The Murals." Lecture at Museum of Modern Art, New York, November 16, 1990. Available online at http://www.mamfa.com/exh/oroz1996/hh_article.htm.
73. Hamill, *Diego Rivera*, p. 182.
74. Hayden Herrera, *Frida: A Biography of Frida Kahlo*. New York: Harper and Row, 1983, p. 107.
75. Rivera, *My Art, My Life*, p. 180.
76. Selden Rodman, *A Short History of Mexico*. New York: Stein and Day, 1982, p. 131.
77. Hamill, *Diego Rivera*, p. 172.
78. Hamill, "Viva Rivera!" p. 61.
79. Quoted in Patrick Marnham, *Dreaming with His Eyes Open: A Life of Diego Rivera*. New York: Knopf, 1998.
80. Rivera, *My Art, My Life*.
81. Hamill. "Viva Rivera!" p. 61.
82. Valero, Javier Barros. "Foreword." In *Diego Rivera*, edited by Linda Downs and Detroit Institute of Arts. New York: W.W. Norton, 1986, p. 7.

For More Information

Books

Pete Hamill, *Diego Rivera*. New York: Abrams, 1999. An entertaining biography of the artist that devotes a lot of attention to Rivera's personal life and Mexican history. It also features many reproductions of Rivera's best-known murals, sketches, and easel paintings.

Hayden Herrera, *Frida: A Biography of Frida Kahlo*. New York: Harper and Row, 1983. Although this critically acclaimed biography is about Rivera's wife, it tells Rivera's story as well.

Laura Baskes Litwin, *Diego Rivera: Legendary Mexican Painter*. Berkeley Heights, NJ. Enslow, 2005. Middle school and high school students are the intended audience for this Rivera biography.

Diego Rivera, *My Art, My Life*. New York: Citadel Press, 1960. This autobiography tells the story of Rivera's life in his own words.

Bertram D. Wolfe, *The Fabulous Life of Diego Rivera*. NY: Stein and Day, 1963. Wolfe worked as an assistant to Rivera on some of his most famous mural projects, so this biography provides many interesting insights and anecdotes.

Periodicals

William Weber Johnson, "The Tumultuous Life and Times of the Painter Diego Rivera," Smithsonian, Feb. 1986. Discusses the controversy that surrounded Rivera's work and life.

Saronne Rubyan-Ling, "The Detroit Murals of Diego Rivera," *History Today,* April 1996. Provides interesting details on Rivera's work on the *Detroit Industry* murals, which many scholars regard as his masterpiece.

Phyllis Tuchman, "The Great Rivera," *Town and Country,* April 1999. Provides a brief overview of Rivera's life and career.

Web Sites

American Masters website. "Diego Rivera." (www.pbs.org/wnet/americanmasters/database/rivera_d. html). This profile of Rivera is based on an episode of PBS's "American Masters" documentary series.

Diego Rivera Mural Project (www.riveramural.com). A Web site devoted to Rivera's mural work in California in the early 1930s.

Virtual Diego Rivera Web Museum (www.diegorivera.com). Extensive web site featuring a wide range of resources on Rivera and Frida Kahlo, including biographical information, film interviews and home video footage, and art images.

Index

Picture Credits

About the Author

Kevin Hillstrom has written and edited reference works on a wide range of subjects, including American history, international environmental issues, current events, and art and culture. In addition to writing *The Cold War* (2006), he has served as co-author of the six-volume *The World's Environments* (2003-04), co-editor of the nine-volume *The Industrial Revolution in America* (2005-06), and series editor of the Defining Moments American history reference series.